HOW TO USE T

In this Series

How to Apply for a Job
How to Apply to an Industrial Tribunal
How to Be a Freelance Journalist
How to Be a Freelance Secretary
How to Be a Local Councillor
How to Be an Effective School Governor
How to Become an Au Pair
How to Buy & Run a Shop
How to Buy & Run a Small Hotel
How to Choose a Private School
How to Claim State Benefits
How to Communicate at Work
How to Conduct Staff Appraisals
How to Counsel People at Work
How to Do Voluntary Work Abroad
How to Do Your Own Advertising
How to Do Your Own PR
How to Emigrate
How to Employ & Manage Staff
How to Find Temporary Work Abroad
How to Get a Job Abroad
How to Get a Job in America
How to Get a Job in Australia
How to Get a Job in Europe
How to Get a Job in France
How to Get a Job in Germany
How to Get a Job in Hotels & Catering
How to Get a Job in Travel & Tourism
How to Get into Films & TV
How to Get into Radio
How to Get That Job
How to Help Your Child at School
How to Invest in Stocks & Shares
How to Keep Business Accounts
How to Know Your Rights at Work
How to Know Your Rights: Students
How to Know Your Rights: Teachers
How to Live & Work in America
How to Live & Work in Australia
How to Live & Work in Belgium
How to Live & Work in France
How to Live & Work in Germany
How to Live & Work in the Gulf
How to Live & Work in Hong Kong
How to Live & Work in Italy
How to Live & Work in Japan
How to Live & Work in New Zealand
How to Live & Work in Portugal
How to Live & Work in Saudi Arabia
How to Live & Work in Spain
How to Make a Wedding Speech
How to Manage a Sales Team
How to Manage Budgets & Cash Flows
How to Manage Computers at Work
How to Manage People at Work
How to Manage Your Career
How to Master Book-Keeping
How to Master Business English
How to Master GCSE Accounts
How to Master Languages
How to Master Public Speaking
How to Pass Exams Without Anxiety
How to Pass That Interview
How to Plan a Wedding
How to Prepare a Business Plan
How to Prepare Your Child for School
How to Publish a Book
How to Publish a Newsletter
How to Raise Business Finance
How to Raise Funds & Sponsorship
How to Rent & Buy Property in France
How to Rent & Buy Property in Italy
How to Retire Abroad
How to Return to Work
How to Run a Local Campaign
How to Run a Voluntary Group
How to Sell Your Business
How to Spend a Year Abroad
How to Start a Business from Home
How to Start a New Career
How to Start Word Processing
How to Start Your Own Business
How to Study Abroad
How to Study & Learn
How to Study & Live in Britain
How to Survive at College
How to Survive Divorce
How to Take Care of Your Heart
How to Teach Abroad
How to Travel Round the World
How to Understand Finance at Work
How to Use a Library
How to Use the Internet
How to Work from Home
How to Work in an Office
How to Work with Dogs
How to Write a Press Release
How to Write a Report
How to Write an Assignment
How to Write an Essay
How to Write Business Letters
How to Write for Publication
How to Write for Television
How to Write Your Dissertation

Other titles in preparation

How To...

USE THE INTERNET

A practical introduction for all computer users

Graham Jones

How To Books

Contents information

Please note: The case histories in this book are fictitious, though they represent what is actually happening on the Internet. Any resemblance of the characters or companies in the case histories to real persons is entirely coincidental.

Cartoons by Mike Flanagan

British Library Cataloguing-in-Publication data
A catalogue record for this book is available from the British Library.

First published in 1996 by How To Books Ltd, Plymbridge House, Estover Road, Plymouth PL6 7PZ, United Kingdom.
Tel: Plymouth (01752) 735251/695745. Fax: (01752) 695699.
Telex: 45635.

Note: The material contained in this book is set out in good faith for general guidance and no liability can be accepted for loss or expense incurred as a result of relying in particular circumstances on statements made in the book. The laws and regulations are complex and liable to change, and readers should check the current position with the relevant authorities before making personal arrangements.

Produced for How To Books by Deer Park Productions.

Typeset by Concept Communications (Design & Print) Ltd, Crayford, Kent.
Printed and bound in Great Britain by The Cromwell Press, Broughton Gifford, Melksham, Wiltshire.

Contents

List of Illustrations

Preface

Most people know very little about the Internet because most people are not using it. Yet every day on TV, radio and in the press we see references to the Internet. You could be forgiven for thinking that you have fallen asleep for a while and that something new and revolutionary has swept by you.

Don't worry, you are not alone; the Internet has passed most people by — so far. Even though at the end of 1995 there were about 35 million people hooked up to the Internet, that leaves quite a few thousand million who are not!

Even so, the Internet is a real revolution in communication; there is little doubt that its development is as important in human terms as the introduction of language. It is as important as that.

WHO THIS BOOK IS FOR

This book is aimed at anyone who wants to use the Internet, or who already uses it and wants to become more proficient in working with the system. Whether you use the Internet for business, education or pleasure, this book will help. That's because, unlike other books on the Internet, you will not find endless pages of jargon or descriptions of how to use Internet computer programs. Instead, this book deals with the down-to-earth, practical matters of getting what you want out of the Internet.

WHY YOU SHOULD READ IT

If you want to find out how to access the plethora of information on the Internet, or you simply want to find out how to use it for fun, this book is for you. You will find out how to save money using the Internet and how to ensure that your children do not gain access to some of the more controversial areas.

It will also help you to communicate, in business or socially, in the coming years. Experts agree that by the end of this century — just four years away — using the Internet will be just as common as picking up the telephone. If you want to keep up to date and communicate in the future, this book is for you.

WHAT THE BOOK DOES

It provides practical, down-to-earth advice. It shows you by example how to gain access to the material you want, and shows you what you can do with the Internet, using case histories. No other book, yet, on the Internet takes this kind of approach.

If you join me and the millions of other users on the Internet, you will be amazed at the material you can get quickly, easily and far more cheaply than any other way.

The Internet is a crucial tool for business and education as well as for pleasure. This book will show you how to make sure that your time on the Internet is used to its best advantage.

Feel free at any time to send me your comments.

Graham Jones
gjones.aspect.@pop3.hiway.co.uk
or, 100016.245@compuserve.com

(If you have never encountered 'code' like the lines above before, they are my electronic mail 'addresses'!)

IS THIS YOU?

Businessperson
Student
Journalist
Scientist
Government worker
Academic
Teacher
Computer user
Researcher
Writer
Designer
Salesperson
Shopper
Illustrator
Doctor
Parent
Traveller
Communicator
Course tutor
Manager
Hobbyist
Advertiser
Self-employed
Manufacturer
Financier
Video maker
Marketer
Publisher

1
What is the Internet?

The Internet is the name given to a collection of computers around the world that can be conncctcd to each other over the telephone line. The Internet itself does not exist as a discrete entity; it is not like one of the many other computerised **database** services, like CompuServe or FT Profile. These are commercial services, run to make a profit. The Internet, however, is a random collection of people, companies and organisations all joined together through the telephone system.

As you will find out later in this book, you too can provide services on the Internet. All you need are:

- a **computer**
- and a **telephone line**

and you are away.

You don't need permission and you don't need any kind of legal approval. You can literally provide services on the Internet from your back bedroom — as many people already do. In essence the Internet is simply a collection of computers that can easily link to each other and swap information.

WHERE DID THE INTERNET COME FROM?

Although we have only recently seen 'the Internet' appear on TV and in the media, it has actually been around for quite a while.

The American origins

The Internet began life in America in the late 1960s, with just four computers owned by the Department of Defense. They were known as **ARPAnet** — the Advanced Research Projects Agency network. To confuse the issue, the network changed its name later in the 1960s and then back again later!

The idea was to swap information between the different sites of the Agency so that in the event of an atomic bomb falling on one of the computers, the Department of Defense would still have access to vital information. Sending information across a small network like this meant it was secure, compared with sending computer data stored on tape across the country in an envelope.

The benefits of this network system soon became apparent to other agencies within the American government. This led to the introduction of **MILNET** — the Military Network — in the early 1980s. Essentially this network evolved from the ARPAnet system which was being used by military personnel as well as defence researchers.

Development by universities

Meanwhile, other groups of computer users were connecting their machines so that they could exchange information.

At Duke University students set up a system called **USENET** — a network built and organised by the users themselves, hence the name. This allowed students to swap information without restriction: no one had set up the USENET system on their own behalf and so there were no external controls.

Before long the professors and lecturers did not want to be out-done, so the first academic network came into being in the early 1980s. This was called **BITNET** and linked the City University of New York with Yale University. The network got its name from the nickname given to the need for exchanging information quickly: Because It's Time.

The American Government was aware of all this networking going on and decided to invest in the technology by establishing funding for the National Science Foundation's own network which became known as **NSFNET**. This was a nationwide educational network linking universities and academic research establishments and quickly enabled scientists to swap data and increase the speed with which work could be completed.

Not to be outdone, British universities established **JANET**, the Joint Academic network, linking together academics across the UK.

'Gateways' give birth to the Internet

By the late 1980s academics were swapping information internationally because it was possible to link into these individual networks using **gateways**. These had been developed by commercial organisations which had been employed by the American National Science Foundation to improve its own network.

These gateways are special systems that enable people on one network to access information on another network. In fact it was the development of these gateways that really gave birth to the Internet, the international network of computers and other networks, all linked together so that information can be exchanged between two machines, anywhere in the world.

The information superhighway

The Internet has seen the most rapid development in the 1990s. American Vice President Al Gore saw the importance of, as he dubbed it, the **information superhighway**. He approved funding for additional network services in the USA and the publicity he brought the networks meant that the Internet had come of age.

The World Wide Web

Another important development came in 1990 from the CERN laboratory in Switzerland, the European Laboratory for Particle Physics. It developed the most rapidly growing part of the Internet, known as the **World Wide Web**. This allows graphics and even video to be moved across telephone lines, bringing even more possibilities to the Internet.

The Internet's expansion

In the past few years the Internet has grown at an amazing pace, and it continues to expand at rates which defy the predictions of the pundits. The fact that most people in the world are still not connected means that the expansion will continue for some time. The number of providers of services on the Internet is currently doubling every three months. In the middle of 1994 there were just 100 services on one small corner of the Internet; by the middle of 1995 that had mushroomed into more than 25,000.

Now it's not just academics, students and government workers who provide services on the Internet. Today, companies the world over provide services and information. It has grown from a four-computer network aimed at avoiding problems due to a nuclear attack into a highly important communications tool for all of us.

WHAT ARE THE CAPABILITIES OF THE INTERNET?

The Internet is capable of much more than most people imagine. Media coverage of the Internet has not been helpful as it gives the impression that it is a collection of computers that are crammed full of pornography; that it is only really used by children; and that if we allow it to continue unchecked we shall totally corrupt every youngster in the land. This has led to politicians in the USA attempting to get Federal controls over the Internet, and to church leaders in the UK talking about the potentially 'devilish' harm of the Internet.

The 'corruption' controversy

Such debates, while probably necessary, make people believe all sorts of things about the Internet which are far from the truth. True you can obtain all kinds of pornography on the Internet, but you can also get much of the same material from your local newsagent's top shelf or from the local licensed sex shop. Even the seedier pornography on the Internet is available in Britain without having to use your computer, say the watchdogs. The Internet doesn't provide anything that you can't get already, though admittedly it does provide easier and far less embarrassing access.

If all you want from the Internet is access to sexually titillating pictures and pornographic literature, fine. You won't be alone as the sexual areas of the Internet attract hundreds of thousands of users. Yet there are millions more people using other parts of the Internet, exploiting its other capabilities.

Access to information

The origins of the Internet lie in the exchange of information and today that is still one of the most important aspects of the network. You can gain access to almost every kind of information that you could possibly wish to. You want to know about pubs in London? Well, there are reviews of them available at the click of a button. You want to know about your nutritional state? Thanks to the Internet you can have your own nutritional status calculated within a few minutes on the phone. You'd like to know what's on at a theatre in a town you will visit on holiday? There it is on the Internet.

Education through the Internet

It's not just practical information that you can get like this. There are educational services too. You can take degrees over the Internet, learning from on-line tutorials, having group discussions with others studying the same subject. It's just like going to university, except that you don't have to travel from your own front room and you can do the studying when you want to, rather than sticking to some rigid timetable.

The Open University, for instance, offers courses over the Internet, as do many other educational establishments.

There are also more informal ways of studying, such as using the encyclopedias and other learning materials that are available. This allows you to research your own chosen subject quickly, and certainly more cheaply, than buying expensive text books of which you only read a few pages.

Business use

As well as information and education, the Internet is increasingly about business. Many firms now have their own Internet 'presence', a place where you can visit them. In this way they can publish their brochures and sales information for you to pick out the precise details you want. That's more efficient than popping down to a local store to find that they only have last year's brochure and it hasn't got the details on the product you want to buy and the price list isn't up to date. On the Internet gaining access to such information is almost instant. You can compare products and services from other companies far more quickly than trudging up and down the High Street.

Shopping by Internet

Some businesses are providing more than information. You can ask them questions about their products and services, to get detailed information that a store-based sales assistant might not know. You can, in some instances, place orders using credit cards or debit cards, or by opening an account with the company. Shopping by Internet is well and truly here. In fact you could have bought this book direct from the Internet, since there is an Internet Bookshop that can get you any book in print.

The social side

As if this were not enough, the Internet provides more. There is a wealth of social life on the Internet. Groups of people 'chat' using the system, sending messages using their computer keyboard; you can even use the Internet as a very cheap telephone, making international calls at local rates legally. If you want, there are Internet dating services, allowing you to find your perfect partner.

WHAT CAN YOU DO WITH THE INTERNET?

Whether you want love, a long chat with your family in Australia at cheap rates, to learn biology to degree level, promote your business, go shopping, or just broaden your knowledge, the Internet can do it. It can give you the news as it happens in many instances, provide you with the minutest details on many topics and even allow you to send your family photos to Great Aunt Matilda in Hawaii. The Internet is highly capable and that's why so many people are interested in it.

The Internet's many uses

With the Internet you can:

- Find out information.
- Send messages anywhere in the world within seconds.
- Make international phone calls at local rates.
- Take part in video conferences at local rates.
- Go shopping.
- Sell things.
- Publicise your business.
- Get your personal problems answered.
- Obtain free programs for your computer.
- Take part in international discussions.
- Catch up on the news — as it happens.
- Study for a degree.
- Find a romantic partner.
- Get unusual questions answered.
- Consult financial advisers.
- Receive electronic newsletters on almost any subject.

- Listen to live radio programmes from different countries.
- Write direct to the President of the USA.
- Check out company financial details.
- Read press releases.
- Read books.
- Get legal advice.

And on and on and on.

As you can see, the Internet provides easy access to a whole host of information and services, all for the cost of a local telephone call. To see how capable the Internet really is, the following case histories give you a taste of what's possible.

CASE HISTORIES

Graphic designer works wonders

Martin is a graphic designer who runs his own agency based in an office at the bottom of his garden. His clients are big international 'blue chip' firms and he works for their offices in many countries, particularly in Europe. His main line of work is in designing advertisements that are used in glossy magazines. He started using the Internet to help his business a couple of years ago. He says that the Internet has boosted his income, made him more efficient and helped his customers reduce their costs.

Before Martin started using the Internet, he relied on air courier companies to deliver his work around Europe. This was expensive and took time. Even the fastest courier service took a day, and some of his clients could only be reached in three days using the fastest and most expensive service. This meant his costs of working were relatively high and the speed his work could be delivered was comparatively slow, even though it was the fastest method of delivery.

Martin's customers used him because he was good at his job and offered high standards of service. But other graphic designers in Europe offer the same. One advantage of using Martin was that all the advertisements around Europe would have a common theme, providing the company with an international identity. Using different designers in different countries could cause differences, his customers thought. But the attraction of having someone in each country would mean that faster delivery times could be achieved.

Martin decided to use the Internet to stave off the threat of his clients saving time by using local suppliers. When he has completed his designs on his computer he simply sends the material through the Internet to each customer's offices around Europe. He can also send a message, invoices and so on at the same time. This is cheaper than air couriers and it saves time: the material is at the offices of his customers within minutes, rather than days. That pleases his customers; as does the fact that he has been able to reduce his prices because he is no longer paying for air couriers.

Martin has also found another benefit for his customers. By using the Internet he can find out information on their competitors or on the market situation for their products. He does this once a month and prepares a short report for his clients, free of charge. That increases his level of service to the companies and helps ensure he will be retained as a supplier.

Young mother gains qualification

Sally is a young mother who has two small children: Ashley who is five and at school and Kirsty who is three and at nursery school three mornings a week. Sally worked for a few years after graduating in psychology from university. Now she wants to use her free time when the kids are out of the house to further her education.

Sally's husband, John, has a computer at home because he sometimes brings work from the office to do in the evenings. He has said Sally can use the computer whenever she wants. Sally decided to try the Internet and find out what was available.

Searching on psychology subjects she discovered that there is a postgraduate diploma in child psychology available. This can be studied by people who have already studied psychology and want to specialise. The diploma can be studied over the Internet. Learning materials can be obtained from the college offering the course and messages can be sent to the tutors. Once a month there is an Internet tutorial, where the lecturers and students talk to each other in a group discussion.

Sally finds that using the Internet as an educational method is much better than a correspondence course. With a correspondence course you can put the materials to one side and forget them. But with the tutorials on the Internet she has an appointment with her teachers, so she has to study in the meantime. This discipline means that she really *does* study.

Sally has also found that she can boost her studies by accessing other areas of information on the Internet. She can find out extra details on every aspect of her course and can ask questions of other Internet users if she has any difficulties. So even if she doesn't know who to ask, someone, somewhere using the Internet has been able to answer her difficult questions!

CHECKLIST

- The case histories show that anyone can use the Internet.
- You can use the Internet for business or for education, among many other uses.
- No single Internet user uses the system in the same way as any other. That is one of the delights of the Internet; it really can be all things to all people.

DISCUSSION POINTS

1. What might you use the Internet for?
2. Could your business be on the Internet?
3. Could your family benefit from access to the Internet?

2
What do I Need to Use the Internet?

Gaining **access** to the Internet is two-fold:

- You need some **physical equipment**. This is dealt with in this chapter.
- You need an **opening** into the worldwide network of computers that is the Internet. In the next chapter you will be able to find out about the companies that provide you with this.

To gain access to the Internet you need some basic equipment:

- **computer**
- **modem** (device for connecting computers to phone lines)
- **printer**
- **telephone service**.

CHOOSING A COMPUTER FOR THE INTERNET

To get into the Internet you need a computer. This will change. In the next couple of years you will not need a computer at all. Already television manufacturers are looking at ways you can access the Internet through your television, bringing you more easily into a world of information than is possible using Teletext services like Ceefax or Oracle. Companies are also developing special telephone devices that will allow you to gain access to the Internet using a specially adapted telephone. One such device is already on sale in Europe and is likely to sell for around £350. So if you are wary of computers and are prepared to wait, in a couple of years you will not need one to access the Internet. In the meantime, though, you do.

What type of computer?

The type of computer you have is not really important. Whether you have a standard personal computer (PC), a Macintosh computer, an Amiga or any other type of machine doesn't really matter. All of them can gain access to the Internet. Indeed, the networks of machines that make up the Internet are of every conceivable type.

Speed

However, the **make-up** of your computer *is* important. The amount of data that you will extract from the Internet will affect the time you spend on the telephone. A slow computer will increase the time taken for the work to be done, thus increasing your telephone bills. If you want to be sure that your work is done quickly on the Internet you need a fast computer.

Fast computers depend on two things:

- the speed of the machine itself
- and the amount of memory it has.

The **speed** of the machine is the speed with which the heart of the computer — its main **microprocessor** — can perform its functions. This speed is calculated in the number of cycles per second the microchip can perform. A 'slow' computer will only function at 16 million cycles per second, or 16Mhz. A fast computer will function at more than 120Mhz. The faster the processor, though, the higher its cost. If you want to access the Internet you should buy a computer that has the fastest processor you can afford.

If you already have a computer it may be possible to upgrade the machine, but since this varies widely you should ask a local computer dealer if it is possible for your particular computer.

Memory

Memory falls into two areas:

- the memory the machine uses to perform its **functions**
- the memory on which you **store** your data permanently.

Both types of memory are important when considering access to the Internet.

Function memory

The memory that the computer uses to perform its work is known as **RAM**, which stands for **Random Access Memory**. This memory is stored on microchips. The higher the amount of RAM your computer has, the better. For a number of technical reasons, as your computer works the amount of memory it sees in the microchips is reduced. This means that if you only have a small amount of RAM, you can soon run out. The computer either stops working altogether, or functions very slowly indeed.

To avoid this you should have a computer with as much RAM as you can afford. Most personal computers are sold with RAM that can store four million parcels of computer information, called **bytes**. Hence the jargon says that the machine is a 4 Megabyte device, or 4Mb. This is really the minimum you should consider. Having a machine with 8Mb of RAM is better and if you can afford more, get more.

If you already have a computer, a computer dealer can often add memory to your machine. Having a large amount of RAM means your computer will function at top speed. Less RAM means it will be slowed down, even if it has a very fast processor.

Storage memory

The part of the computer that stores information in a permanent form is the **hard disk**. Almost every computer these days has a hard disk inside the main case. Such disks can store considerable amounts of information. Nowadays a 'small' hard disk can store 40Mb of data, but most machines would have a hard disk with over 100Mb of space.

Of course, the larger the hard disk's capacity for storage, the higher the cost. Once again you should consider buying a computer that has the largest hard disk capacity you can afford. You will be storing pages you obtain from the Internet and you will be surprised at how quickly you can run out of space if you only have a small hard disk.

If you already have a computer, a dealer can usually change your hard disk for a larger one.

So your computer should be:

- fast
- have the highest amount of RAM you can afford
- have the largest hard disk capacity you can afford.

If you already have a computer you should upgrade all of the parts that you can so that your machine is improved. Accessing the Internet will be slow and therefore more expensive than necessary if you do not have the smartest, fastest computer you can afford. Don't skimp on your equipment as you will regret it in the future when you become hooked on the Internet!

Screen

Your computer will need linking to a **screen** or **monitor** so that you can see what you are doing. Some computers come with an integrated screen, but for most you need to purchase a separate screen and plug it in. Sometimes you can use a television as a monitor.

Your screen is an important part of the computer set-up you need to access the Internet. You will be sitting in front of this monitor, using it as your window into the worldwide communications network. Therefore having a monitor that is less than good will not be helpful. There are three things to consider when buying a monitor for Internet access:

- size of the screen
- speed of the screen
- colour capability.

Screen size

Monitors come in all shapes and sizes. The size that is advertised, like televisions, is the diagonal distance between two corners. An average computer monitor is 14 ins. However, they vary from 9 ins up to a whopping 37 ins. For access to the Internet don't go lower than 14 ins. If possible, get a 19 ins screen as this will give you a much bigger window into the Internet and enables you to perform tasks more quickly. The bigger the screen, the more information you can get on it and hence the faster your connection time, thus reducing your telephone bills. If you have a small screen you will need to stay connected for longer.

Naturally, large screens cost more money. So once again buy the biggest you can afford.

Screen speed

The speed of the screen is important. The monitor has to translate information coming from the heart of the computer and convert it into an image you can see. If this conversion process is slow, your connection time will be increased. People with very fast computers often miss out because they have monitors that are very slow.

So when buying a screen make sure it is fast. This will be a combination of certain technical items, including the speed with which the main computer processes the **video signals**, and the speed with which the monitor can interpret them. This often depends upon the amount of **video memory** in your computer. If possible, buy a machine with the maximum amount of video memory allowed. This will speed up your work on the Internet, helping to reduce phone bills.

Colour capability

Much of the Internet is in colour, so buying a black and white monitor would lessen your effectiveness and reduce your enjoyment. Get a colour monitor; they are only marginally more expensive. However, the *number* of colours the screen can display is important. Screens can display either:

- 16 different colours
- 256 colours
- several thousand colours
- or almost 17 million colours

Get a screen that displays at least 256 colours. If your screen displays thousands or millions of colours, you will be able to change the display so that only 256 are shown. If you have higher amounts of colours on display, you slow down the monitor and that increases your connection time to the Internet.

Other computer devices

There are some extras which you should consider when setting up computer equipment for Internet access. These include:

- **mouse**
- **compact disc** access
- **sound cards**
- **microphone**

- **loudspeakers**
- **video cards.**

Mouse

Your computer will need a 'mouse'; this is a small, hand-held device that allows you to position the pointer on the screen. All computers come with mice these days.

If you have an old machine you will be able to use the Internet without a mouse, but your work will be speeded up if you get one.

Compact disc access

If your computer has a slot for using computer compact discs, known as **CD-ROMs**, this will be useful, although it is not essential to using the Internet. Many computer magazines have cover-mounted CD-ROMs that are full of useful programs and other material. Much of this can be used in gaining access to the Internet.

If you don't have a CD-ROM slot, don't worry; you will still be able to use the Internet. But if you do have a CD-ROM slot you could increase your enjoyment by having access to much more material that you can use.

Sound cards, microphones and loudspeakers

A sound card is an additional piece of computing technology that you can add to your main machine. These cards are printed circuit boards that can be plugged into the main processing board of your computer. Sound cards allow your computer to process sound signals more quickly and efficiently than the main part of the computer.

If you intend to use the Internet for any work that will involve sound, such as listening to far-flung radio stations, or sending voice messages, or using the Internet as a replacement telephone, you will need a sound card. You will also need a microphone to allow you to talk into the computer and record your voice, or other sounds.

If you are using a sound card you will be able to play your sounds through a loudspeaker that is present in the computer. However, you will have better quality sound, especially if you are using the Internet to make telephone calls, if you add a *pair* of loudspeakers to your machine.

Video cards

If you intend getting into the higher end of the Internet, where you can watch video clips or take part in video teleconferences, you need a specialist video card. These allow the moving images to be processed rapidly, thus improving your access to the Internet. If you rely on just your computer's basic video capabilities, your connection time will be dramatically increased.

So if you want to use the Internet for any video work you should add some kind of extra video capabilities. Your computer dealer will be able to advise you as to which additional card will be best for your machine.

CHOOSING A MODEM FOR THE INTERNET

A modem is a small device that connects a computer to a telephone line. The telephone system mostly uses a different kind of technology to computers. The modem is a sort of translation device that allows computer-based information to be transmitted along telephone wires. The modem also translates incoming information from telephone wires that can then be used on a computer.

Internal and desktop modems

Modems come in all sorts of shapes and sizes.

- **Internal modems** fit neatly inside your computer. They slot into the main processing board of the computer.

- **Desktop modems** sit alongside your computer and you can stand your telephone on them.

- Tiny, **hand-held** modems can be used on the road with portable computers.

The type of modem you choose is largely a matter of personal taste. If you don't have much desk space, you might want an internal modem. If you want to use a modem with a number of different computers you might want a desktop variety that you can pick up and move about. If you have a portable computer you will want the tiniest device available to make transporting it in your briefcase easy.

Most people, though, opt for desktop modems. They are easier to connect than an internal modem since you don't have to take the computer apart. However, they cost slightly more because you have to pay for the casing. An internal modem is essentially a desktop modem without a case. Deciding on the style of modem is one thing, but sorting out exactly which model to buy is another!

The modem you choose will be a compromise between the facilities offered and the amount of money you have available. A cheap modem will have fewer facilities than an expensive one. The factors you need to consider when choosing a modem include:

- speed
- error correction capabilities
- compatibility with computer programs
- fax capabilities
- network ability.

Speed

The speed of a modem is the most important factor you need to consider. You should buy the fastest you can afford.

Modem speeds are measured in terms of the number of distinct items of computer information they can send per second down a telephone wire. This is known as **bits per second** or **bps**. Currently the fastest modems operate ar 28,800bps. If you intend doing a lot of work on the Internet, don't settle for anything slower. The faster the modem, the quicker your Internet connections and the lower your phone bill. If you can't afford a 28,800bps modem, the next fastest alternative is 14,400bps. Other modems exist at 9,600bps, 2,400bps, 1,200bps, and even the snail-paced 300bps.

Accessing the Internet shouldn't really be considered with modems at speeds of less than 9,600bps. Some people do use old modems at slower speeds, but they pay for it with higher than necessary telephone bills. The cost of fast modems is more than outweighed by the cost of additional telephone charges when using a slow modem. Get the fastest modem you can afford and you will save considerably in the long run.

Error correction capabilities

Because modems are translating computer and telephone data constantly and because there is 'noise' on telephone lines, there is the potential for error. Most modems now have error correcting capabilities built in.

Your Internet work will be boosted if your modem offers automatic error correction as it will reduce the problems caused by the current state of technology. If you don't use error correction you may find you have to repeatedly return to the Internet to access information that was interrupted by noisy phone lines. This will only increase your phone bill.

Compatibility with computer programs

Modems built by different manufacturers — and there are several hundred of them — vary in the way they work. So the instructions that computers provide to them need to be compatible with the particular brand of modem. Dealers selling modems will be able to tell you whether your programs are compatible.

Generally, the leading brands are popular with all software. The only problem is that the 'household names' in the modem world tend to be slightly more expensive than similar unknowns, because the company's reputation is built into the price. However, if you wish to be compatible with all the communication programs that you will use — and as you will see in the next chapter you will collect them! — buy a leading brand. This will save you time and effort in the future, or worse still having to buy another modem next year to remove conflicts.

Fax capabilities

Many modems now have fax capabilities built in. Such **fax-modems** are useful and only cost slightly more than a standard data modem. Fax-modems mean you can use your computer as a fax machine. If you are buying a modem to get onto the Internet, buy a fax-modem and you will benefit. It is cheaper than buying a separate fax machine — and you don't need to buy fax paper.

Network ability

If your computer is to be **networked**, that is connected to other machines in the same location, you need to buy a modem for every computer unless you buy one that is **network capable**. Such modems are much more expensive than ordinary single computer modems, but vastly cheaper than buying a modem for each computer. If you want a number of people to access the Internet from different computers, make sure your modem is network capable.

CHOOSING A PRINTER

Even though the Internet is electronic communication, you will need a printer. You will be surprised at the amount of information you can retrieve, and reading it all on your screen can be time-consuming and tiring on your eyes. It is far better to print it out and read it more leisurely.

Computer printers come in a variety of kinds. Although there are other kinds, popular varieties are:

- dot matrix
- inkjet
- laser.

Buy the best quality printer you can afford.

If you can afford a colour machine, so much the better. This will enable you to print out the coloured items from the Internet and see them in print as you saw them on the screen. Colour inkjet printers are comparatively cheap and are often available as a package deal with the computer.

Laser printers are the most expensive, but provide the best quality.

Dot matrix printers are not always easy on the eye. So if you are going to print out a lot of information from the Internet — and you probably will — avoid low quality, cheap, dot matrix printers.

BUYING YOUR INTERNET COMPUTER SYSTEM

Buying a computer system that you can use for the Internet is easy.

- You can get an excellent system on every high street.
- You can buy a system via mail order.
- You can use a specialist computer dealer, often based in business parks or in offices out of the centre of town.

The method you choose will depend on a variety of factors, but if you are new to computers you are best to buy from a dealer or high street store, rather than mail order.

If all you want to do is upgrade an existing system or add to your computer set-up, mail order is fine. Indeed, mail order will probably provide the lowest prices, but if you have never used a computer before, beware: you will be left alone once you have made the order. Next day some boxes arrive and you are faced with all the unpacking and connecting.

Whilst this is also true for high street stores, you can always pop in for

DATE	NUMBER	TIME ON	TIME OFF	REASON

Fig. 1. A log for your Internet access.

advice or even ask for an installation service, which some companies offer.

Computer dealers offer the best level of service, but you pay for it with higher prices. Fortunately, there is very competitive pricing now in the computer industry and you should be able to buy a complete **Internet kit** comprising a computer, printer, modem and all the necessary programs pre-loaded into the machine as a package. Look out for such packages advertised in the national press, or ask your local dealer for a quotation for such a system.

CHOOSING A TELEPHONE SERVICE FOR THE INTERNET

Most people will be connected to British Telecom lines in the UK, or to an equivalent master network elsewhere. If you are connected to a cable television telephone service, your access to the Internet could be free (see below).

Of course, there are competitors to British Telecom. You can use Mercury lines, for instance, or businesses may benefit from Energis, a relative newcomer to the telephone business. In addition there are telephone account systems from companies like AT&T, the major American telephone company. These allow you to charge your telephone costs to a special account, rather than having to pay your own telephone supplier for the call.

Finding the cheapest phone company

Advertising by competitors to British Telecom often emphasises the differences in call charges. However, simple comparisons are not always as clear as they might seem. For business users, British Telecom offers a range of discount packages that compete very well with the call charges from other services.

Because many people become hooked on the Internet you can find yourself on the phone for long periods. For this reason you should investigate all the options available to you from all the telephone service suppliers in your area. Only by calculating the likely times you are going to use the Internet, and the likely length of your connection time, will you be able to work out which is the cheapest company to use for the telephone line.

You should monitor your Internet usage on a periodic basis. This will enable you to swap your telephone service if necessary, to attract lower call charges. Keep a log of all your Internet access, including time of day, length of call and so on, in order to get the best out of the Internet at the cheapest possible price. (See Fig. 1.)

Cable TV phones

Some cable TV companies now provide telephone line services. Sometimes calls to local numbers on such services are free. If you can access the Internet using a local connection, your call time will be free, making this a highly cost-effective way of using the Internet. Indeed, it may even be possible to use Internet telephone techniques to make international calls for nothing! If you have a cable TV operator in your area investigate the possibility of using their telephone service.

The downside is that your number is not listed in a local directory as you no longer have a connection to the main British Telecom network, even though you can call any BT number.

CHECKLIST

- Accessing the Internet requires a certain amount of equipment and a telephone line.
- Choose a telephone line service that provides you with the cheapest possible call charges for your pattern of use.
- Choose a computer system that enables you to connect to the Internet for the shortest possible time to achieve your aims. This means the fastest computer you can afford that has considerable amounts of memory and plenty of storage space.
- Equally, your modem should be the fastest you can afford.
- Fast computer equipment and the cheapest telephone line service will enable you to enjoy the Internet for the least cost overall.

DISCUSSION POINTS

1. Why should you choose a fast computer?
2. Why might a cable TV telephone service be useful?
3. How much computer memory is 'enough'?

3
How to Access the Internet

If you already have a computer set-up capable of accessing the Internet, as described in chapter 2, you will probably be raring to go and **surf the net** as the **net junkies** would say.

As you can see, before you even start exploring the world of the Internet you are faced with a whole new language. Things will get worse! The world of Internet access is full of jargon, so much so that many people who would benefit from the Internet are put off trying to use it. This jargon creates a mystique which prevents the Internet from gaining wider popularity. Before you even attempt to get onto the Internet, you need to come to terms with the jargon.

UNDERSTANDING THE INTERNET JARGON

The basic terminology of the Internet includes:

- Access provider
- Client
- Dial-up
- Domain
- Email address
- FAQ
- FTP
- Host
- HTTP
- IP
- Mailbox
- POP
- POP3
- PPP
- PSTN
- Server

- SLIP
- TCP
- URL
- WWW

Sadly, all of these terms face you the instant you decide to join the Internet. Even though magazine articles trumpet the simplicity of the Internet, many people are put off because of the considerable amount of terminology that is presented to new users from the outset. Until new ways of accessing the Internet arrive — and they will soon (see chapter 10) — you simply have to face up to the task of understanding the jargon. It isn't that difficult, actually; it just looks different and smacks of computer whizz-kid stuff.

Access provider

This is the company (sometimes called a **service provider**) that sells you a method of getting your computer connected to the rest of the Internet. These companies have computers that are permanently linked to the Internet using expensive telephone lines that are permanently 'open'. Such **leased lines** cost about £10,000 a year to rent and allow a company with a computer to keep their machine permanently linked to the Internet.

When you want to get onto the Internet for half-an-hour or so, you call their computer on a special telephone number and then connect to the Internet through their permanent telephone line. In return, you pay the company providing you with such access to the Internet a fee.

Client

You will see this term in magazines, books and on the Internet itself. It means the computer program you are using to do the particular work on the Internet you want. So your electronic mail program is your 'email client', for instance. Whenever you see the word 'client', just think of it as a program.

Dial-up

When you are not permanently connected to the Internet using a leased line, you make a special telephone call through your modem. You are literally dialling up an access provider and hence your connection to the Internet is known as a **dial-up connection**; you are not permanently hooked up, just for the length of the telephone call.

Domain

This is a bit like a town or city name in an ordinary postal address, except that it is a description of where a computer is somewhere in the world. The 'domain' identifies a particular part of the Internet.

Email address

This is your address on the Internet. It is the specific pointer to you, just like your home address in the postal system. When someone sends electronic mail to your email address, it is automatically routed to your **mailbox**. Your email address will include the **domain** and the **host** in it. For instance, my email address is: gjones.aspect.@pop3.hiway.co.uk

FAQ

Because the Internet started in America and still gets the greatest use from Americans, things get shortened! **FAQ** is simply shorthand for **frequently asked question**. Whenever you access the Internet, or read an Internet magazine, you will see 'FAQ' all over the place. The reason is, lots of people ask lots of questions!

FTP

This is another piece of American shorthand and it means **file transfer protocol**. You need never worry about it. The file transfer protocol is the technical way in which the computers talk to each other to transfer information. It is invisible to you and you don't have to be concerned about it. The only problem is, you will see the acronym FTP all over the place in books and magazines and you think you have to know about it. Just take it as read that if you are using the Internet, you are using FTP!

Host

This is the **section** of the domain in which your mailbox resides. In other words it is the computer your access company uses to connect you to the Internet.

HTTP

This is yet another piece of shorthand that stands for **hypertext transfer protocol**. Hypertext is a computerised method of improving the way you can use the system. By pointing your mouse to a word or phrase in a document you are viewing and then clicking the mouse button, you can be transferred to more information on your selected topic. You need not worry about HTTP, since it is automatic.

When you are trying to find information on the Internet, though, you will find you type HTTP a great deal of the time. This acronym provides an instruction to your computer on how to look for information on the Internet. Other than typing it endlessly, you need not worry about this piece of jargon.

IP

This is the **Internet protocol**. It is an internationally agreed set of computer instructions which ensure that machines on the Internet can connect to each other and transfer information. Ignore this term. If you are connected to the Internet, IP is working. However, in magazines, manuals that accompany programs that connect you to the Internet and so on, you will see IP. Forget it.

Mailbox

This is a storage area on your access provider's computer (host) in which information addressed to your email address is stored.

POP

Once more this is shorthand jargon and means **point of presence**. This is typical computer-speak: it means where someone is! In other words if an access provider is based in London they have a London POP. Similarly, if an access provider, like mine, is in Newbury, they have a

Newbury POP. However, access providers try to have POPs in many places around the country. This means you can get connected to the Internet using local telephone calls. You will see advertisements in computer magazines from access providers which proudly state things like '120 POPs'. This means they have many places in the UK where you can connect to their system and gain access to the Internet.

POP3

Just to confuse things, this has nothing to do with 'point of presence'. This is a method for sending electronic mail messages. It stands for **post office protocol number 3**. You don't need to worry about it, except that you will occasionally see it in email addresses.

PPP

This stands for **point-to-point protocol**, which is the way in which two computers at different sites talk to each other. It is entirely invisible and you have no need to worry about it. Access provider advertising, though, often contains statements such as 'we provide PPP'. It all makes sense to those in the business but to us mere mortals it's technical jargon that we need not worry about. Forget it!

PSTN

This is yet more jargon you will see in advertisements or listings from access providers. You will see statements such as 'our Internet software can be used on PSTN'. Nonsense, what they mean is their software can be used over the telephone! Computer whizz-kids never use one word when four will do. PSTN stands for 'public switched telephone network'!

Server

A **server** is a large computer that is one of the main machines on the Internet. Just think of the word as being synonymous with computer.

SLIP

Yet more jargon which you will see from access providers and that you can happily ignore. It is the way in which computers talk to each other and stands for **serial line Internet protocol**. You will see this in advertising and in magazine articles. If you talk to anyone about the Internet they may drop into the conversation that they can provide you with **SLIP** or **PPP** access methods. In fact, SLIP is an old method which is now being replaced mostly by PPP. It doesn't matter which method your computer uses; it's all invisible to you. Yet more jargon you can ignore.

TCP

This stands for **transmission control protocol** and is the computer's programs' method of communication with the Internet. You sometimes see the abbreviation **TCP/IP**. You need something that is capable of both TCP and IP (see earlier) if you are to connect to the Internet. If you successfully connect to the Internet you are using TCP/IP. However, you will see this abbreviation a lot in magazines, adverts and manuals. Just ignore it.

URL

This is shorthand for an **address**, that is the location of the material you are looking for. **URL** stands for **uniform resource locator** and it can be used to identify an individual computer, or a particular piece of information on a specific computer. When you see addresses printed in magazines or books, these are URLs. You need to understand what a URL is because you will be expected by your program to enter the URL of the information you are looking for.

WWW

This stands for **World Wide Web**, sometimes called **W3**, and is the name given to the newest part of the Internet that is capable of providing high quality graphics and video.

The vital jargon

As you can see, there is a great deal of jargon associated with the Internet. Thankfully you can ignore almost all of it. Just remember that:

- you need an access provider
- your host is almost always the access provider's computer
- your email address allows people to send material, such as messages, to your mailbox, which is a storage area on your access provider's computer.

Other than that, don't try understanding the jargon, it's a waste of your time which you could use much more usefully, trawling the Internet for the information you want.

TRYING OUT THE INTERNET

You might want to have a sneak preview of the Internet before joining up, to see if you get on with it and find anything of interest. Happily, there are a variety of ways you can do this. These include:

- trial offers
- cybercafés
- computer stores.

Trial offers

Trial offers are frequently found in computer magazines. Most computer magazines have cover-mounted disks and these frequently include the programs you need to access the Internet. Usually an access provider has let the computer magazine distribute software that provides anyone with the ability to get onto the Internet for a limited number of days. So you might get a 28-day trial offer on the cover of a magazine. This will allow you to see what is available, free of charge.

If you like what you see you can carry on using the software after the payment of a fee to the company that provided it. However, as you will see in the next section, this might not be a good idea as the company's location may be too far from your home or office. Even so, using these trial offers is an excellent way of seeing what is on the Internet.

Visiting cybercafés

There are a number of these around the UK, mostly in the large metropolitan areas such as London and Bristol. The number is growing steadily, though. Cybercafés, like traditional cafés, are places where you can go for a drink and a snack but at certain tables there are computers connected to the Internet. You can have a coffee, dabble in using the Internet and chat to the staff who will help you use the programs and find your way around the systems. Cybercafés are great places to learn about the Internet.

If you only occasionally want to access the Internet, it can often be cheaper to go to your local cybercafé than to join up with an access provider for your own Internet account. Cybercafés are popping up all around the UK, and are advertised and listed in the specialist magazines on the Internet.

Visiting computer stores

Many computer dealers and high street computer retailers are connected to the Internet. They will be able to provide demonstrations for you. Some shops even have special promotional days, where there are large-screen demonstrations of the Internet. It is worth looking out for such special promotional days. If local shops do not provide them, it is still worth going into a local computer dealer and asking for an Internet demonstration.

At computer shops you will also find **Internet kits**. These are packages which contain Internet programs and a time-limited amount of free access using a national access provider. Sometimes such kits also include a modem. These are often cost-effective ways of exploring the Internet.

CHOOSING AN ACCESS PROVIDER

Before you can connect to the Internet you need an access provider, unless you are going to spend many thousands of pounds on a leased line and have your computer permanently connected to the Internet. If you are going to get the maximum out of the Internet you will be making regular telephone calls. Hence it is best to use an access provider which has the same national dialling code as your own. This means all your access to the Internet will be made with local call charges, thus keeping your telephone charges lower than if you used a provider further afield.

Access providers advertise their services in computer magazines and in the specialist Internet magazines that are sold in most high street newsagents. Some magazines also contain lists of access providers. These magazines include:

- *Internet*
- *Internet and Comms Today*
- *.net*
- *Net User*
- *What Net.*

The listings provide a whole host of information that will help you make your mind up. The things you need to consider are:

- location of the access provider
- extent of access
- registration fee
- on-going costs
- access speeds
- modem-to-user ratio
- software
- support
- other services.

Choosing the right location

You want an access provider which is local. If you cannot find one that has the same telephone dialling code as you, look for one of the large national suppliers and see if they have a POP which is close to you. Often a town doesn't have an access provider, but one of the large national firms will have a local POP. You will be able to spot this from the magazine listings.

Choosing the right access

Some access providers only provide email facilities, allowing you to send and receive electronic mail but not use any other part of the Internet. Others allow you full and unrestricted access to everything, including some of the more dubious sites, such as those containing extreme views, pornography and so on. Some access providers limit the areas you can visit, excluding anything they view as pornographic — in other words they act as unofficial censors. If you have children and want to restrict the dubious areas choose a provider who has some kind of censorship. This is not always listed so you will have to ask the company direct.

Paying the registration fee

Almost every access provider charges an initial registration fee to cover the costs of setting up your mailbox and providing you with the necessary computer programs to get going. Registration fees vary enormously. Some companies do not charge an initial set-up fee, but then provide less in the way of support, for instance. Others charge very high registration fees to provide you with your own dedicated system so that everyone in a large office can use the Internet. Hence registration fees can vary from nothing, right up to £1,500. For most users, though, the initial setting up charges will be between £10 and £25.

Budgeting on-going costs

The Internet itself is free of charge. However, access providers who are permanently linked to the Internet will charge you a fee for connecting. The usual method is to charge you a monthly fee which allows you unlimited access to the Internet. You can dial up and stay on line for as long as you like and you are not charged any extra. Equally, if you do not use the Internet one month you are still billed for the monthly fee.

Monthly fees vary from about £8 up to £15. Some companies offer a discount if you pay your costs for a full year in advance. Discounts for a full year's payment in advance vary, but are around ten to 15 per cent. If you intend using the Internet at least once a week, it's best to opt for annual payment if you can afford it.

Some companies do not have monthly or annual charges, but charge you according to the amount of time you are actually connected. These firms have an hourly rate and you are automatically billed for the length of your connection time. If you are only going to use the Internet for a short period of time this may be the cheapest option, but if you use the Internet a lot this can work out to be quite an expensive method of connection.

Choosing your access speed

As has already been mentioned, you should opt for the fastest modem you can afford. However, your Internet access is actually limited by the speed of the modem of your access provider. If you have a very fast modem working at 28,800bps, and your access provider only has a 14,400bps modem, your work speed will be halved to match that of the slowest modem. The magazine listings show what speed modems the access providers have. Be sure to pick an access provider which has the fastest modems possible as this will help reduce your phone bill.

Getting the right modem to user ratio

If the access provider has a number of modems it means more people can connect to the Internet through their system. If they only have one line and one modem, only one person can connect at a time. This means you will be frustrated at your attempts to connect as you will keep getting an engaged signal. Choose an access provider which has only a few users per modem. This way you will be less likely to have connection problems.

Choosing the right software

To look around the Internet you need computer programs — software — that follows all the protocols (TCP/IP, SLIP, PPP, etc). An access provider usually gives you the software as part of the registration process. Check that you will get the appropriate software. As you will see later in this chapter a variety of software is available. One or another may be more appropriate to your needs, so ensure the access provider uses the software you want, if you have a specific reason.

On the whole, though, the vast majority of users can use the software that comes from the access provider with no trouble at all. However, some access providers do not produce the software and you need to locate it yourself which can be troublesome. So choose an access provider which lets you have some software.

Finding support

Some access providers give only a little technical support and assistance. Others provide a 24-hour support. If possible choose a local access provider which has good levels of support. Someone who only provides support for a couple of hours in the morning may be no good to you if most of your Internet work is going to be in the evening.

Other services

If you are in business you may want to promote your products and services on the Internet. If you were to set up your own Internet computer this would cost from around £15,000 to do properly. However, access providers usually provide a low-cost method of having your own Internet 'presence', often for around £25 a month. If you want some Internet presence of your own in the future, choose an access provider which has the ability to provide you with the space on their machine. The listing and the advertisements usually explain whether this is possible.

Questions to ask an access provider

As you can see, there is a lot to consider when choosing an access provider. Other things you might like to ask when contacting a company include:

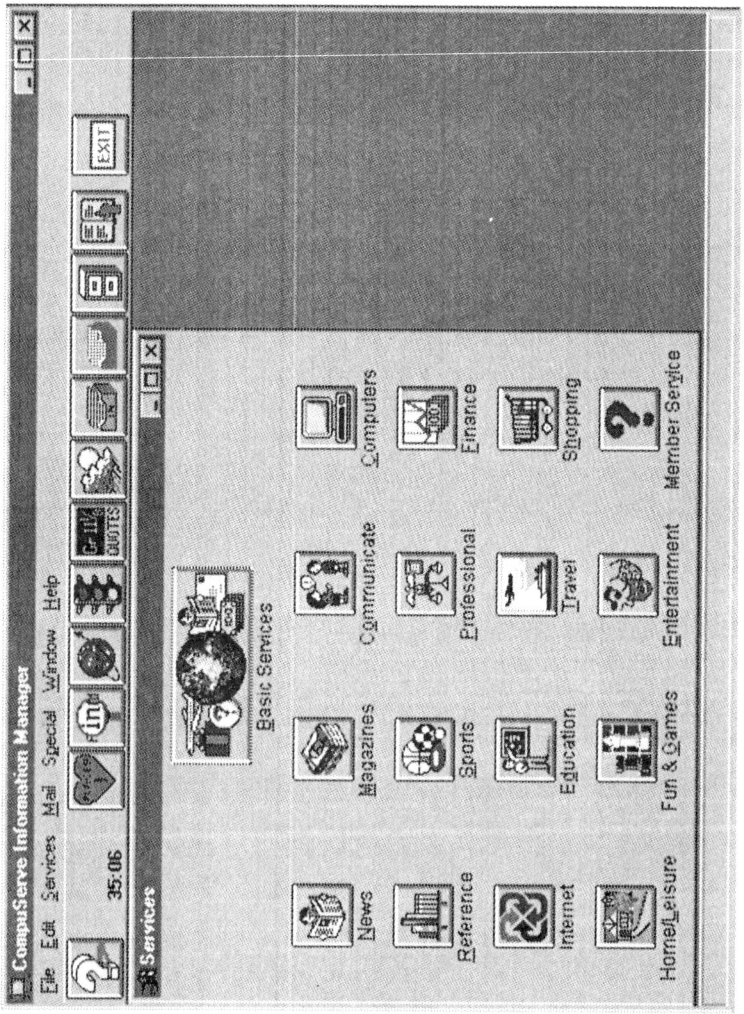

Fig. 2. CompuServe is one of the on-line access points to the Internet.

- How long have they been in the Internet business?
- How long have they been in the computer business?
- How many staff do they have working on their Internet business?
- Do they provide Internet training courses?
- How many people use their services?

Answers to these questions will show you how confident you can be in the supplier. If they have been in business for a while, have more than one person working on their Internet business, provide training courses and have many people using their service, they are probably alright. However, you can be an access provider from the spare bedroom; all you need are a computer, a modem and a leased telephone line. But although there are many such good companies, some one-person firms could easily be snowed under and not be able to support you properly if they have thousands of customers.

Asking a few questions will be able to determine whether the local access provider is going to be of real help to you.

USING ON-LINE ACCESS PROVIDERS

Sometimes you do not need to use a local access provider. Instead you can gain access to the Internet using a commercial 'on-line' company. These companies provide their own databanks as well as specialist interest areas, but instead of being on various unrelated networks, like the Internet, all the material is in one central location and is under the control of the owning company. Such on-line firms include:

- America On-line
- Computerlink Information Exchange (CIX)
- CompuServe
- Microsoft Network
- E-world
- UK On-line.

Fig. 3. You can access the Internet from the Microsoft Network.

These firms charge users to access their own databanks and specialist interest groups. The material is censored and highly controlled, but is not as extensive as the material on the Internet. Even so, these on-line information companies do provide access to the Internet. Some provide full access, giving you unrestricted movement around the international networks. Others restrict you to just sending electronic mail.

They usually charge for every second you are connected to the Internet. So if you are going to be a regular Internet user it usually works out to be more cost effective to use the services of the on-line company of your choice for *its* information, and access the Internet using a local access provider.

SETTING UP THE SOFTWARE

Once you have an account with an access provider, and you have your Internet software, you will need to set it up. This can be traumatic for some people if your service provider hasn't pre-configured your software for you. In fact, the process of setting up the software can be so confusing and time-consuming that some people have given up trying to connect to the Internet from the outset. This is a real pity since there are so many benefits of the Internet.

Help with setting up

Happily, some access providers set up the software in advance for you. Others will visit your office or home and load it onto your computer and configure it ready to work. When you join up with an access provider ask them if the software is pre-configured and ready to run when they send it to you on disk. If it isn't ask them if they provide a setting-up service, for which they will charge extra, of course. Most access providers will do one or the other.

Doing it yourself

If your access provider is unable to set up the software for you, be prepared for an irritating time sitting in front of your computer. Setting up the software is not easy, unless you are confident with computers. Internet software is not generally intuitive to set up. So, even though you will be keen to get on and travel the international networks, be patient. Read thc manuals and the instructions carefully. If you do not understand something, call the access provider for information. Don't attempt to configure the software unless you are confident you know what you are doing.

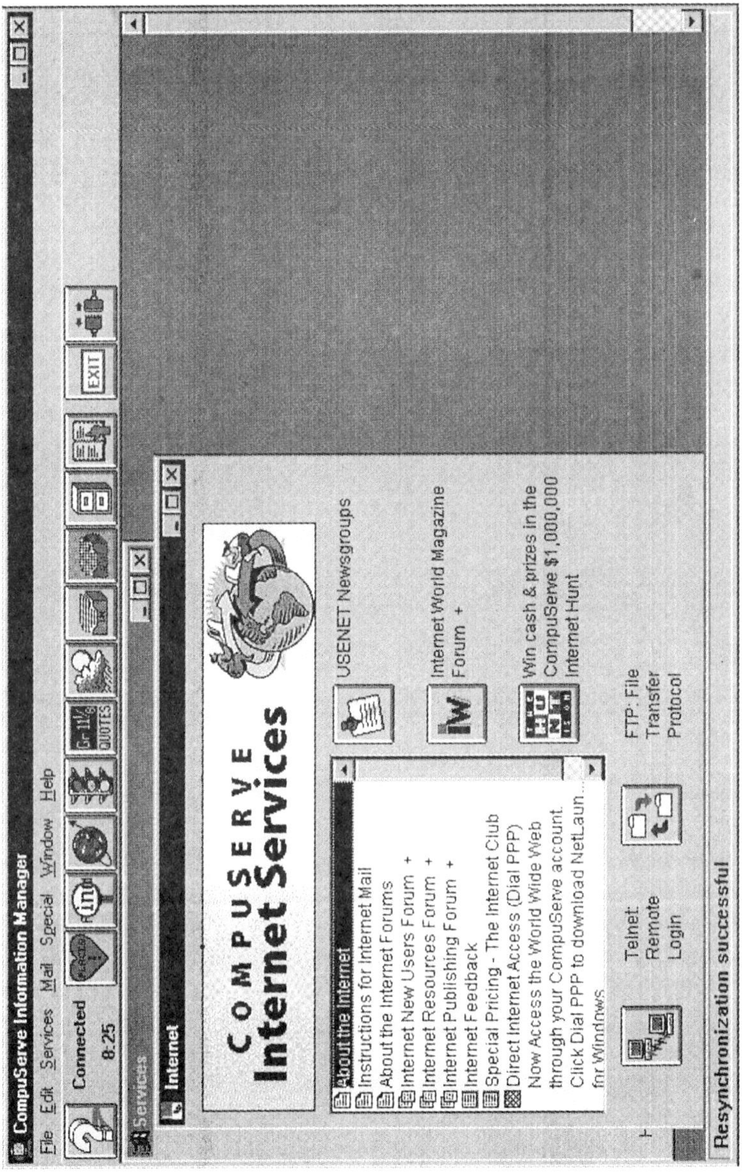

Fig. 4. You can access the Internet via CompuServe.

To get the software running you need to enter various options, according to your computer and modem set-up, plus you may also need to enter some numerical codes which provide your unique identification on the Internet. If you are at all confused, contact your access provider.

Happily, many people will avoid this troublesome start to the Internet. If you do have to configure the software yourself, one good thing is that having done it once you shouldn't have to do it again!

USING THE SOFTWARE

The programs that you get from the access provider will allow you to:

- send and receive electronic mail
- transfer data across the networks
- extract information from databanks
- read news items.

Sometimes you are provided with just one program that does all this work; other companies let you have a variety of programs.

Programs to fit your needs

In any event you have to connect to the Internet with a program that supports the various protocols, then use another program that allows you to do the kind of work you want to do at that particular time. You might want to send electronic mail, so you need to use the **electronic mail program**. Or you might want to read pages on the World Wide Web and you need a **Web Browser** program to do that. Your access provider will let you have the programs for the facilities you can use, but you usually need to remember that accessing the Internet is a two-part process:

- firstly, your access program (SLIP or PPP program) dials up your access provider and connects you
- then you use your Web Browser or email program.

Mostly, the whole of this is automated and you need not worry too much. However, your connection to the Internet is not finished until you have stopped the SLIP or PPP program. Even if you exit from your Web Browser or your email program, you will still be connected to your access provider's computer, running up your telephone bill. Never forget to disconnect otherwise you will unnecessarily increase your phone bill.

Downloading programs

There is a wide variety of programs available and once you are connected to the Internet you will find that you can **download** other programs, often free of charge, to your own machine.

- Downloading is the process of transferring something from one computer on the Internet to your own.

- The opposite process, **uploading**, is when you transfer something from your computer to another one on the Internet.

If you download other Internet programs you will be able to compare them to the one provided by your own access provider. However, be careful. This can lead you into all sorts of uncharted territory and could destroy the files that your computer uses to access the Internet. So only use different Internet programs to the one your access provider let you have if you are technically competent.

SIGNING ON

To get on to the Internet, and connect to the information superhighway, all you need to do is follow the instructions provided by your access provider. Sometimes these are not all they should be!

You need to start your main access program (SLIP or PPP program) to get connected. You may be asked for your account details and often you will need to enter your **password**. The first time you connect you will be allowed to choose your own password. Choose one that you will remember easily, otherwise you could be locked out of the Internet.

Once connected you start the program that allows you to do the work you want. You will start either your email program, or your Web Browser, or your newsreader. You can have them all running at the same time, if you want. Then it's up to you what you do, where you go and how long you do it for. Later chapters will help you with this aspect of your Internet activity.

CASE HISTORIES

Group for the handicapped improves communication

People Care is a group of handicapped individuals who work from home. They all use computers for their work, but are not always capable of using the telephone; some are profoundly deaf, other suffer from speech defects which make telephone communication difficult. The members of People Care are spread across the UK.

They recently joined the Internet using the services of a national access provider. This meant they could all dial in using local telephone calls to a nearby POP, which kept their call charges to a minimum. Also, they only wanted electronic mail facilities so they could use their computers as their principal communications tool with each other. This saved some money on setting-up charges as they didn't need all the other software to get to places like the World Wide Web. Setting up a dedicated electronic mail system would have cost thousands of pounds for People Care. Now they have been able to do this cheaply using the Internet.

Print and publishing group goes on-line

Steve runs a large print and publishing company and decided to use the Internet to expand its work. The company mails its brochure over the Internet and allows customers to send work for printing over the Internet to its own 'presence'.

Steve opted for full Internet access with a large local access provider. This company also rents out space on its computers for local firms to have their own Internet presence. In this way, Steve's customers can go direct to his pages on the Internet, without having to send electronic mail and wait for a reply. This means Steve can put important information on his space at the access provider and his customers can retrieve it when convenient.

CHECKLIST

- Starting out on the Internet is not as easy as you might think. Without proper planning and reading all the literature that accompanies your programs, things can go wrong from the outset.

- Once everything is set up, however, access to the Internet is straightforward. You can easily be put off by the setting-up process if you are not careful.

- Choose a local access provider and this will save you money in the long run.

DISCUSSION POINTS

1. When might you choose a national access provider instead of a local one?

2. Why might you choose an access provider with restricted access to the Internet?

3. What would be your key considerations for choosing one local access provider rather than another local one?

4
Communicating on the Internet

One of the principal uses of the Internet is communicating with other people. You can do this in a variety of ways. These include:

- email
- netchat
- newsgroups.

USING EMAIL

Electronic mail is great — providing you know people who can receive it! If you don't know anybody else who uses the Internet, your ability to exploit electronic mail will be somewhat limited.

However, you can still send electronic mail, even if you don't know anyone with an Internet access account. That's because you can send email messages to people even if you don't know them. For instance, say your bank appears on the Internet (a number do); you can send the bank an email message to say how grateful you are they have come into the 20th century and started to use modern technology. Or you could send an email message to the President of the USA (the correct email address is 'President@whitehouse.gov'). So even if you know no other Internet users, you can still send email messages.

Business uses

If you know other Internet users, though, you can send messages that are much more useful. For instance, you can conduct business over the Internet by sending messages more quickly and cheaply than either phone or fax. The reason is that your message will be sent using a local telephone call, providing your access provider has the same dialling code. This means you can send the same kind of information you would put in a telephone call or a fax to your offices, customers or suppliers anywhere in the world for the cost of a local call.

In addition sending the message only takes a few seconds in most instances; if you gave the same information in a telephone call you could waste a lot of time — and spend more money — by asking how the person is feeling, what the weather is like and so on!

Email can, therefore, be a very cost-effective way of communicating for people in business. Another benefit is that you don't have to hang on while the person comes to the phone, nor does your fax machine have to retry three times because the line is engaged, or the machine at the other end has run out of paper. These additional benefits provide greater convenience and reduced costs.

Keeping in touch through email

Even if you are not in business, you can save time and money by using electronic mail for communicating. Say you have family in Australia. Sending email messages between your family in the UK and your relatives in Australia can be fun and is cheaper than using the phone — and more convenient since Australia is eight to eleven hours ahead of GMT! You can send your email messages at your convenience, rather than having to make late-night phone calls.

Planning email use

Whatever reason you use email for, you will benefit from it if you plan your usage. Otherwise you will waste time and that will increase your telephone charges. The two areas you need to concentrate on are:

- **off-line work**
- **address books**.

Off-line work

To save call charges you should always prepare your email messages in advance, that is before you dial up your access provider. In this way you can write your messages and then send them in one short phone call. If you connect to the Internet and then prepare your messages you will be paying for call charges while you are typing your messages. Make sure you prepare messages off line.

Similarly, read your email messages off line. The most up-to-date electronic mail programs allow you to gather in one go all of your email from the computer at your access provider, where your mailbox resides.

The messages are then copied to your computer. You can then end your Internet session and read the messages at your leisure. If you read the messages as they come in, you will waste connection time and increase your costs.

Keeping address books

All email programs allow you to have address books. These are separate files that you keep on your computer hard disk. You store the email addresses of all the people you want to send messages to.

It's a good idea to build up your address book. In this way you can instantly call up someone's address when preparing your messages. This saves you time when sending messages, since you don't have to look up email addresses after you have connected to the Internet.

FINDING EMAIL ADDRESSES

There are a number of ways you can find out email addresses. Some people include them on their business stationery, for instance. Others publish email addresses on their pages on the World Wide Web. Some include email addresses in advertising. Wherever you see an email address that could be useful to you, add it to your address book; it will save you time in the future when you want to send a message. Of course, you can always phone people and ask them for their email address; once you have it, you might never need to phone them again.

If you know that someone does have an email address there are a few ways you can find it using the Internet. Firstly, you can send email messages to other contacts who you think might know the relevant address. They can then email you with the right address. This approach might seem useful, but if you send your email request to a large number of people, you might get a lot of replies back. That means you will waste time collecting your email messages next time you connect to the Internet, thus increasing your call charges.

A simpler way, though not foolproof, is to use the various searching methods on the Internet. The best way is to use **Gopher**.

Gopher

Gopher is a searching device created by computer experts at the University of Minnesota in America. It is a highly sophisticated method of searching the international networks for people, information and so on. To find out an email address you need to go to the following location on the Internet:

gopher.tc.umn.edu

The easiest way to do this is to use your Web Browser program. There will be an option, usually called Open Location or Open URL. This provides you with a box in which you should type the line above, preceded by:

http://

This will link you to the University of Minnesota computer. Then you need to choose the kind of information you are looking for from the list you see on your screen. You can then access lists of addresses and search for the person or company you are hoping to locate.

UNDERSTANDING EMAIL ADDRESSES

An email address can look rather confusing, but they are not as daft as they first appear. Take my email address:

gjones.aspect@pop3.hiway.co.uk

You can actually work out quite a lot from this, if you read from right to left.

- UK identifies the address as being in the UK. Other countries have similar codes: JP is Japan, for instance, DK is Denmark and so on.

- The 'co' identifies the computer where my mailbox resides as being in a company, that is a business site. Other codes include 'com', meaning a commercial on-line service provider, or 'edu' meaning an educational establishment, or 'gov' meaning government. Other such codes include 'mil' for military and 'org' for any kind of organisation. So, the second word from the right shows what kind of person you are.

- The third word, in my case 'hiway', identifies the specific computer on which my mailbox resides. Hiway is the Internet division of Compass Computers in Newbury who provide me with Internet access.

- 'Pop3' identifies me as a 'POP3' mail user. This means my

electronic mail uses the most up-to-date methods of transfer, meaning I can accept all kinds of electronic mail, including those items of mail that have pictures in them.

- The @ sign means 'at'.
- Then 'aspect' is the name of my business, technically my 'host' — the part of the hiway computer that houses my specific mailbox.
- Then gjones identifies me specifically.

So now reading from left to right you can see that my mailbox is

G Jones from Aspect, at the Hiway company in the UK.

Knowing how an email address is put together means you can sometimes guess at an address. For instance, say you want to send something to someone called Bill Bloggs at the BBC in London. You could try:

Bbloggs@bbc.co.uk

or Billbloggs@bbc.co.uk

COMPOSING EMAIL

Writing email is not the same as writing a letter. For a start, the longer the message, the longer it will take to transmit and the higher your telephone bill. For this reason many people write a kind of shorthand in email messages, thus reducing their costs. When writing email try to use short words, short sentences and any possible abbreviations. The shorter your message, the lower your costs.

Using abbreviations

Some common abbreviations are:

- B4 before
- CUL see you later
- FOC free of charge

- FYA for your amusement
- FYIO for your eyes only
- FYI for your information
- IME in my experience
- IOW in other words
- KISS keep it simple stupid
- NRN no reply necessary
- OBTW oh by the way
- OTT over the top
- RSN real soon now
- RUOK are you OK?
- TIA thank you in advance
- TTFN cheerio
- TVM thank you very much.

There are hundreds of such abbreviations and sometimes you need to sit and work out what they mean. If you enter the world of electronic mail, be prepared to see such abbreviations frequently.

Using common signs and symbols

You will also find signs in common usage. These are meant to express emotions in ways that you cannot otherwise do using non-direct contact with other people. Common signs and symbols include:

- :-) happy
- :-(sad

- :-t cross
- :'-(crying
- :-O shocked

There are dozens more, including ones to tell your email recipients whether you have a moustache, whether you wear glasses and even if you have a cold!

SENDING EMAIL MESSAGES

To send an email message you need to use your email program, having composed and addressed the messages off line.

You usually need to add a **subject** line at the top of the page. There is usually a separate box for you to type in. A subject gives the recipient a quick guide to what your message is about. Some email programs will not allow you to send a message until the subject box is completed. If you are having trouble sending messages, type something in this box. Once your message box is completed all you need do is click your mouse button on the box marked **send** and the rest is automatic.

Do not forget to disconnect from your access provider as soon as you have sent the mail, otherwise you will increase your costs unnecessarily.

RECEIVING EMAIL

If no one knows you have an email address, your chances of getting email are slim! Before you can receive email you must tell people your address. So let your friends and colleagues know your email address. If you are in business, add email addresses to stationery and business cards.

Another way of getting email is to let people on the Internet know your address. You can subscribe to mailing lists so that you regularly receive messages of interest to you. To find a current list of mailing lists send an email message to:

listserv@bitnic.educom.edu

Your message should read:

list global

In return you will receive an email message that is a list of all the mailing lists available. It is a very long email message! You can then use this list to access the mailing lists of interest. All you do is send a short message to the relevant mailing list email address and ask to subscribe. You will then receive all the email you want!

READING EMAIL

When you get an email message you might be confused by all the codes at the beginning. This happens if your email program won't allow you to switch off **headers**, as they are called, or if you haven't selected this option.

The header contains a whole host of information which is used by the computers and has no relevance to you. If you can switch off the headers, do so. With headers switched off you can go direct to the main body of the message. With headers switched on you can sometimes miss the beginning of the message and miss important information.

As stated before, it's best to get your email, disconnect from your access provider and then read your mail. If you need to send replies, reconnect to your access provider later; that is cheaper than staying connected and paying extra phone charges.

USING NETCHAT

Netchat is exactly that, chatting on the Internet. It is a bit like a telephone conversation, except that there is no talking; everything is typed on the screen. Also, unlike a telephone conversation it involves more than two people. When chatting on the Internet, hundreds of people can be involved in the same conversation; it is rather like a very large conference call.

Internet Relay Chat

The official name given to chatting on the Internet is **Internet Relay Chat** and is known as IRC. Typing, rather than talking, may seem a slow way of communicating. However, IRC does have some excellent uses. For instance, when the Gulf War was in progress people around the world were able to get instant reports of the fighting from IRC-users in Iraq and Kuwait. This instantaneous, live reporting is only possible with TV or radio — and their reporters might not be in the right place at the right time. With IRC users in every town and city, you can get the news as it happens. Hence when important world events are occurring, many news organisations use IRC as a means of finding out what is going on; so too do governments and political organisations, the military and so on.

IRC also has uses in education; you can connect to a number of people studying the same subject and discuss the topics you are learning about. Indeed, some educational establishments hold tutorials in this way on the Internet. Businesses can hold conference calls in this way as well, saving considerably on telephone charges since everyone will be paying only local call charges.

To get the most out of communicating with IRC you need to understand two things:

- channels
- IRC commands.

Channels

The area of the Internet devoted to chatting is divided up into channels. These are subdivided into four groups:

- public
- secret
- hidden
- string.

Public channels

These are the 'talk about anything' channels. Anyone can join in the conversation and can see what everyone else is saying. Other people using IRC can see what channel you are using and are therefore able to see what subject you are chatting about.

Secret channels

These are the channels that you can join, but only the other people using the channel will know you are contributing. No one else using IRC knows which subject you are discussing, though they know you are using IRC somewhere.

Hidden channels

These are totally private; no one knows you are using IRC unless they are contributing to the same channel.

String channels
These are completely private; you can only join them by invitation. No one other than the people using the channel with you knows you are using the IRC system, except the computer company or organisation that owns the computer. String channels are used for things like educational tutorials.

Using IRC commands

These are special commands that you need to type in during a netchat session. There are dozens of commands, though happily most are sensible. You do not need to be a computer whizz-kid to understand them. All commands are preceded by a slash:

/

hence:

/join

means you want to join a particular channel,

/leave

unsurprisingly means you want to leave the channel.

Other common commands include:

/away Lets other users know you have moved away from your computer but will be back later, so they won't expect a reply to anything they say until you return.

/ignore Allows you to specify that your machine will not receive parts of the conversation from someone you cannot stand! Sometimes people taking part in IRC are obnoxious; this command lets you filter out their conversation.

/me This allows you to perform 'an action'. For instance I could type /me making notes. Everyone else would see on their screens 'Graham Jones is making notes'. In other words, it's a shorthand for typing your name and saying what you are doing.

/msg Allows you to send a private message to one of the other people using IRC. Your message will not be seen by the other people taking part in the conversation.

/signoff This command ends your session with IRC completely.

/who This lets you know who is using IRC.

/whois This lets you know some information about an individual user.

FINDING OUT ABOUT THE CHAT SUBJECTS

Before you can communicate using IRC, you will need to know what subjects are on offer. This depends upon which computer is providing your IRC service. There are a number of IRC computers around the world and the subjects discussed depend on which you are connected to. Also, the usefulness of the discussions varies according to the type of computer providing the IRC service. Some are comparatively slow, meaning that the conversation can be a bit jumbled as all the data is swapped around the world.

Faster IRC providers use a system collectively known as **Undernet**. These IRC providers remove the problem of slow conversations, but they can be very busy since there are fewer of them.

Whichever kind of computer you connect to for IRC, you can find out the subjects on offer by typing

/list

in your IRC program, that should have come from your access provider. If no such program came, you can download suitable programs from the Internet itself. Which program you use and where you get it from will depend upon the computer you are using.

USING NEWSGROUPS

Newsgroups are similar to IRC, except that they are not 'live'. You can send messages to other members of the group, and read the messages and 'conversation' that have taken place since your last visit to the newsgroup. Most newsgroups reside in part of the Internet known as **Usenet**, though not all.

Types of newsgroup

Newsgroups are broken down into broad categories and the first word of the newsgroup's address indicates which category it falls into. Popular categories include:

- **alt** alternative newsgroups, often on sordid or dubious subjects
- **biz** business newsgroups
- **comp** computers
- **news** discussions about Usenet itself
- **rec** recreation, such as sport and the arts
- **sci** science
- **soc** social matters
- **uk** the UK.

Joining a newsgroup

To take part in any newsgroup you have to join, or subscribe. Subscriptions are free, but they are public, so other Internet users will be able to find out which groups you have subscribed to. Hence if you do subscribe to an 'alt' newsgroup on Elvis Presley (there is one) other people will know your little secret!

When you subscribe you will be using your newsreader program that came from your access provider. This will allow you to download the messages in the newsgroup and to reply to particular messages, or contribute original material. Having read the messages you can prepare your replies and reconnect to send them. You will save on your phone bill if you use newsgroups in this way. Staying connected to read messages can take a very long time in some newsgroups because of the large number of messages.

If you do subscribe to a particularly personally important newsgroup, you should dial up every few days, because messages take space on the newsgroup computer. The computer owners therefore delete old messages to save space. For busy newsgroups this is done every three or four days, so if you do not dial up regularly you could miss out.

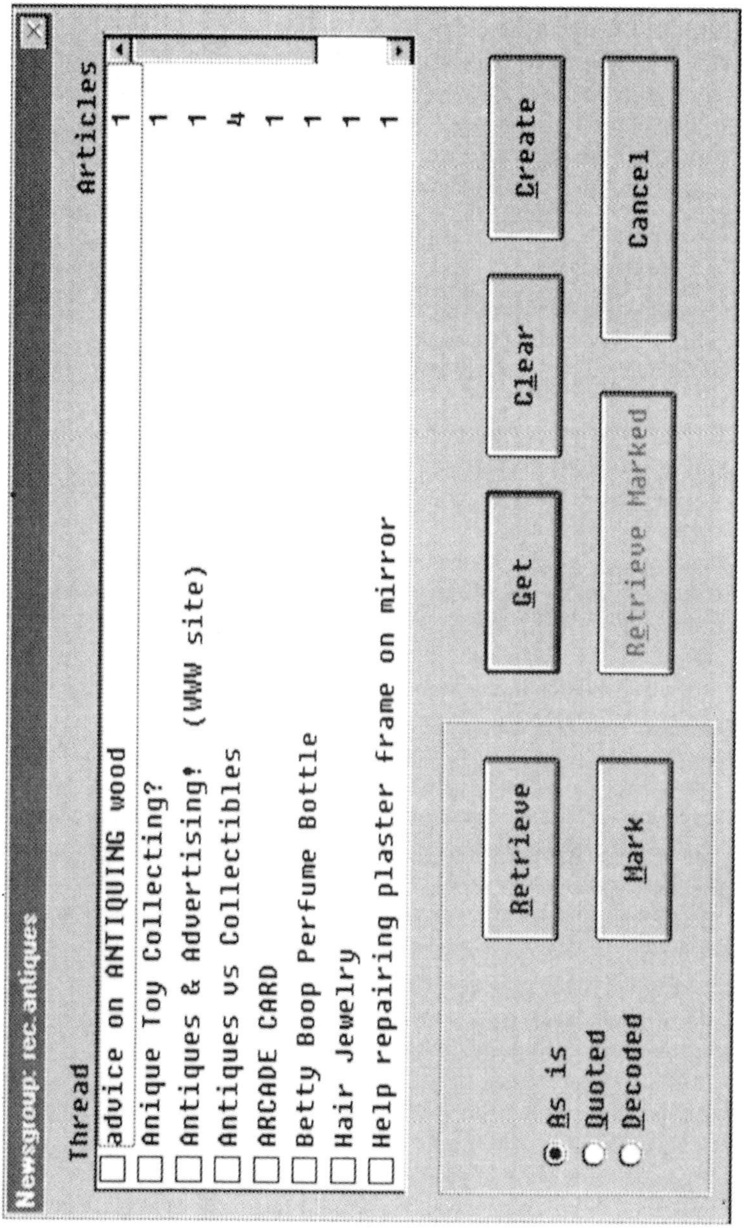

Fig. 5. A typical newsgroup listing.

Finding out about newsgroups

There are thousands of newsgroups and new ones are being formed every day. To find out if there are newsgroups of interest to you there are a couple of options. You can either use your Internet program to search for topics of interest to you, or you can access

news.lists

to find an up-to-date list of newsgroups.

CASE HISTORIES

Family keeps in contact with email

Andy is a disc jockey working on the west coast of America. His programme runs during the middle of the night. That means he sleeps during the day which makes it very awkward to keep in touch with his family back in the UK. When they do have a chance to phone him in the evening, he is asleep. When he is awake, they are asleep or out at work.

Happily Andy is on the Internet and his parents also have a computer at home because his father is preparing the family tree on the machine. By adding Internet access to their machine they have been able to send messages to Andy and he has been able to keep in touch with them. It's quicker than the postal service and cheaper than sending faxes, which is important because his mother and father are retired. Then at weekends, when it is possible to talk on the phone, their calls are shorter because there is not so much news to catch up on, making their phone bills even cheaper.

Sally studies with IRC

Sally, who is studying for her diploma in child psychology, uses IRC once a month. She takes part in a string channel which is used by the university for its tutorials. There are eight people taking the diploma and together they discuss the issues which have occurred during their studies. Then the lecturer asks questions and gets some feedback on how well they are doing. The lecturer also gives advice and sets material for studying before the next tutorial. Since everyone is connected using a local phone call, this is far cheaper for everyone than travelling to the university, or holding a conference telephone call.

CHECKLIST

- Communicating on the Internet is very efficient. Providing you access the Internet using a local access provider, your communications will be less costly than standard telephone calls and faxes because you can communicate around the world for the cost of a local call.

- Whether you use email, or the Usenet newsgroups, it is best to download your messages, disconnect from the Internet, then write your replies and reconnect. You will save time and money if you disconnect and reconnect. Reading on-line can be costly.

- If you use IRC for netchatting, you need to understand the various commands that will ensure you get the most out of the chat channels.

- Whichever way you communicate on the Internet, be sure to learn the shorthand methods of communicating; this saves you typing lengthy items and also saves on your phone bill.

DISCUSSION POINTS

1. How could email improve your life?

2. What newsgroups would you like to subscribe to?

3. How might you benefit from IRC?

5
Getting Information from the Internet

The Internet began life to exchange information, so it is no surprise that one of its main uses is in the distribution of information around the world. Almost every subject area is covered, and if it isn't it's easy to set up your own Internet site that provides the forum for information exchange on that topic. Whether you want to make information available, or obtain information, you can do it.

Using the Internet as a vast international library is very cost effective. In fact, you could not look up some of the information on the Internet in a traditional library. Equally, if you did, it would take days trawling through dozens of reference books. They, of course, would be out of date and your information search would be tiring, expensive and time consuming. With the Internet, however, you can search for literally up to the minute information and you get the material in seconds, often from the only place in the world that has the information on the specific subject you want. There are a number of ways of extracting information from the Internet. These are:

- file transfer
- direct connection to other computers
- the World Wide Web.

USING FILE TRANSFER

One of the most common acronyms you will find when exploring the Internet is **FTP**. This is the Internet's **File Transfer Protocol** and it is the technical way in which files are exchanged between various computers.

When you want information from the Internet, you may well find that it is in a computer file, somewhere in the world, but this file is

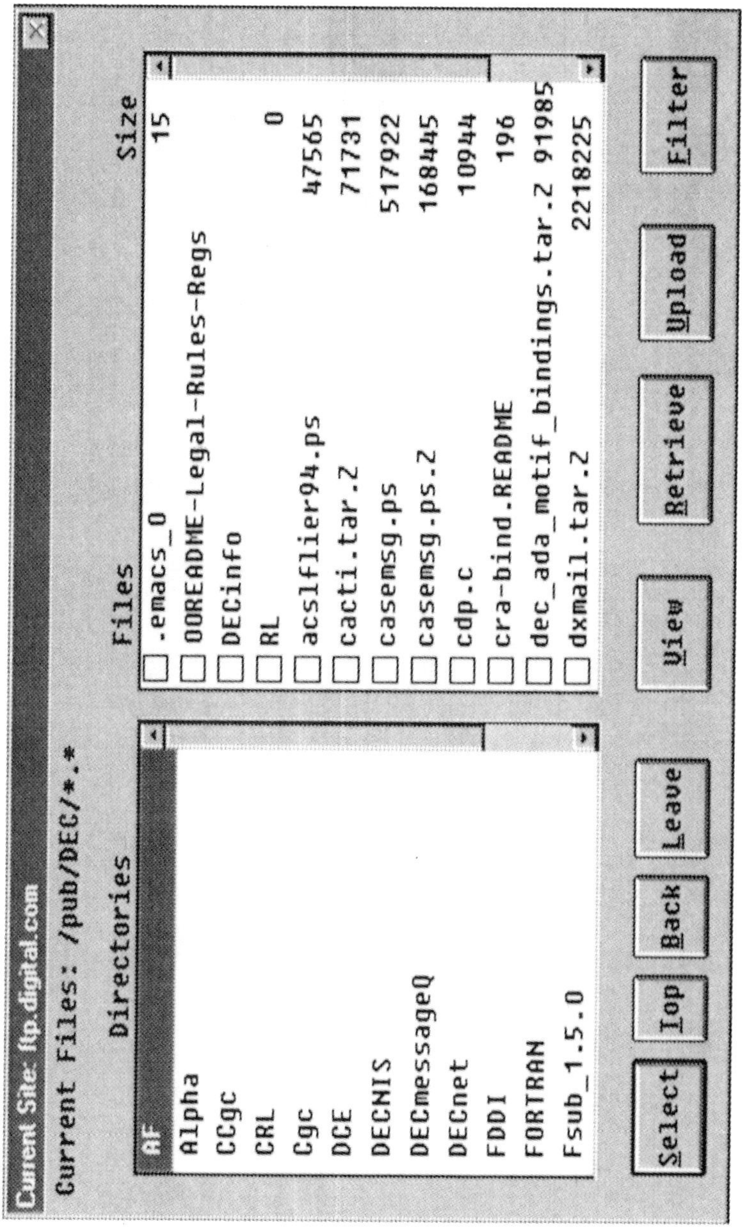

Fig. 6. An FTP session in progress.

unreadable by your Internet access program. However, the file may be readable by other computer programs you have. For example, the information you want may be in the form of a **spreadsheet file**, if it is something to do with finances. Or it might be a **database document**. Often, the files you download using FTP are computer programs in their own right, allowing you to increase the usefulness of your machine. Sometimes the file of information is so large that it is compressed, to be expanded on your own computer once you have downloaded it. In any event you use FTP to get a copy of the relevant file.

Using FTP to download information

You don't have to worry about FTP, it's all invisible to you. However, when using the Internet you will see this acronym quite a bit. Using FTP means that you can find complete files of information relevant to your needs and then download then to your machine. After that you end your Internet session, open the files and use the information for whatever purpose you extracted it in the first place.

USING DIRECT CONNECTION TECHNIQUES

There are some computers that contain extensive amounts of information that you can effectively connect directly to. Your computer believes it is directly connected to this large information-containing computer, much the same way as if you had two computers in your office or study connected to each other. However, unlike two computers in the same room, Internet **direct connection** allows computers thousands of miles apart to link up with each other.

At first sight this seems to be just what the Internet does anyway; but it isn't quite the same. The Internet allows you to access all sorts of computers around the world. The direct connection system allows you to see on your screen exactly what is on the other machine. In other words you can use the directly connected machine as though it were on your own desk. This kind of connection is known as **Telnet** and it is a very popular method of extracting information.

Computers which provide Telnet information are either public or private.

- A public system allows anyone to connect and extract information. One well known one is the Colorado Alliance of Research Libraries (CARL) in the United States. This allows you to connect and search for the specific information you require in over 10,000 academic journals.

- A private system is one to which you need to register, sometimes for a fee. This is worth doing if you are likely to be visiting this particular computer on a frequent basis. You can usually register as a guest to explore the kind of information that is available, for a limited period, so that you can find out if the computer is likely to be of use to you.

USING THE WORLD WIDE WEB

Most people gaining access to the Internet for the first time nowadays will head straight for the World Wide Web for their information. That's because it is the easiest to use section of the Internet and the fastest growing. In fact it is so easy to use you do not need much computer knowledge, if any. You just point your mouse to the information you want, click the mouse button and there it is on your machine. The World Wide Web provides access to an incredible amount of information. Some of it is highly useful, other pieces of information are plainly unnecessary.

Pages

The World Wide Web presents its information in **pages**. These contain headlines, main items of text, pictures, even videos in some instances.

Each page can include **pointers**. These are specially highlighted pieces of text that allow you to jump to another page, even if that page is on another computer elsewhere in the world.

Accessibility

The World Wide Web is very easy to use to find out all sorts of information and if you are new to the Internet this is the place to start. When you hear about people surfing the net this is the area of the Internet they are most likely to use. They can bob about from one information area to another with the greatest of ease. For instance, in one ten-minute surfing session on the Internet I was able to find out information on the following topics:

- The British Chambers of Commerce
- A conference in Vienna on the impact of science on daily life
- A new competition for screenwriters
- The drinks company Allied Domecq

- What's on at the theatre in Vancouver when I visit
- Plus I was able to download a short story!

This all took ten minutes and I was able to achieve it simply by clicking my mouse on the highlighted pointers, sometimes called **hot links**. Also, because it was a ten-minute local call at a weekend, the cost was a mere 9p! You simply could not get all this information for this low price in any other way. The kind of information you can find simply by surfing the Internet is quite amazing.

However, for many people this would be a waste of time. You may want specific information about a particular topic; simply meandering around the Internet would waste your time and increase your phone bill. So you would need a method of going directly to the information you want.

SEARCHING FOR INFORMATION

There are plenty of ways you can search for the kind of information you want. The trick is to plan your search *in advance*. Don't connect to the Internet and then start looking for what you want; you will waste connection time by thinking of the terms you want to look for.

There are three search tools that you will commonly use. These are:

- **Archie**
- **Gopher**
- **Web Searchers**.

USING ARCHIE

Archie allows you to find files that you download to your own computer. It can search complete archives of material, hence its name. Your access provider will probably have let you have a program that performs Archie searches. If not you can use Archie search techniques via the Telnet system. The easiest way is using the Archie system from your access provider. As with all searches, work out what it is you want to look for before you connect to your access provider's computer. That way you will save money with reduced connection times.

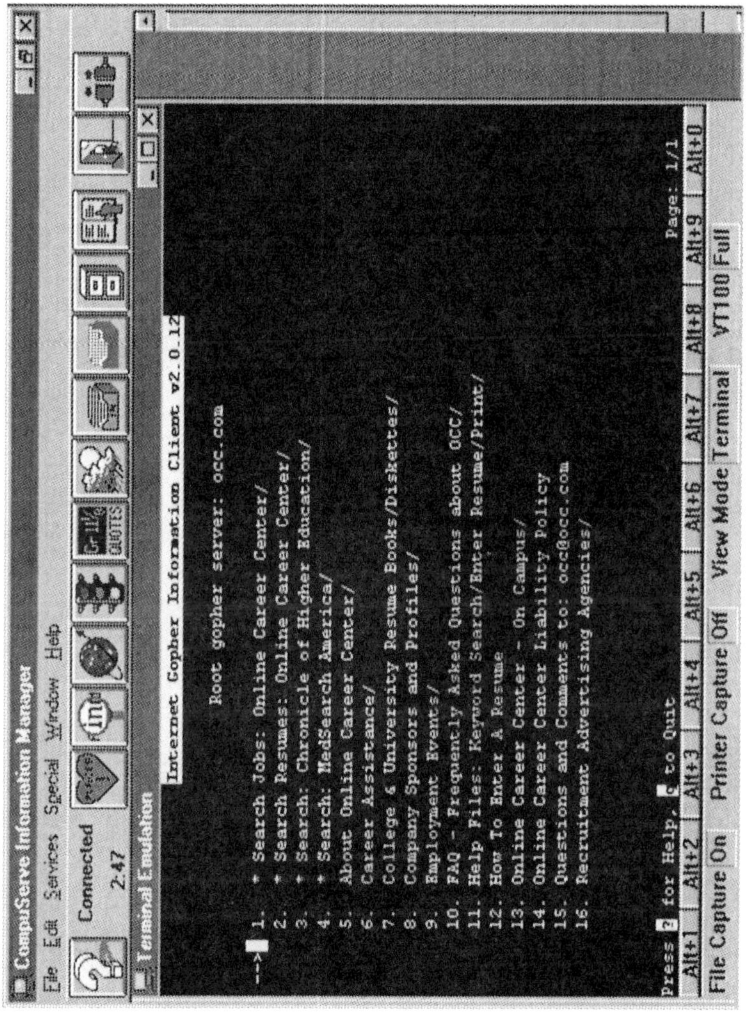

Fig. 7. A Gopher session will look like this.

Four types of Archie search

Archie searches are of four types:

- **Exact** searches are just that; you are looking for exactly what you typed in. This is only useful if you know the name of the file you are looking for.
- **Regex** searches are powerful searches which are best used by computer experts. Unless you know a great deal about the **UNIX** method of computing, forget regex searches.
- **Sub** searches mean you can type in a word which is likely to be contained in the file name you are looking for, but you don't have to worry about whether you are using capital letters in the right place, unlike Exact searches.
- **Subcase** searches only require part of a file name, but they must have the capital letters in the right place.

As you can see, the sub method of searching using Archie is the easiest.

When using Archie you need to use some computer commands to get the material you want. The most common one you will use is

prog

which instructs Archie to search the archives for the material you are hunting.

USING GOPHER

Gopher, introduced in the last chapter, is a highly powerful **search engine**, as these locating programs are called. As well as being very powerful it is also easy to use. It presents the information it finds in a sort of **menu option**. You select what you want from the menu list and this takes you to a further menu with more details on the subject area you have chosen.

Imagine that you want to search for something on cat fleas! Your cat has had a sudden outbreak of fleas and you want to find out if there is anything you can do, beyond what your vet has said.

Using Gopher you can locate veterinary information, then information on cats, then on fleas and then on alternative healthcare methods.

Gopher works in this hierarchical method, taking you ever downwards to smaller and more specific pieces of information. Then when you locate the item you want you can access the information since you are provided with an address of where to go. Often, you can click on the file name you want to reach and you are taken there directly, without having to type in the relevant address yourself.

The many different Gophers

Gopher is not a single program, though. There are hundreds of Gophers around. Each is based on different computers throughout the world and each contains different information on various topics. So, although the Gopher system is very powerful, you need to be reasonably certain of which Gophers are likely to contain the information lists you want.

This is not as difficult as it sounds. For instance, Imperial College in London has a Gopher in its chemistry department computer. If you are looking for anything on chemistry, that seems a good place to start! Meanwhile, if you want information on business in America, the Florida State University College of Business Gopher seems worthwhile.

The availability of Gophers is easy to find out, since you use a Gopher that lists the Gophers! If you can grapple with the hierarchical concept of information, you will easily understand Gopher. The Gopher of them all is the original one at the University of Minnesota, as explained in the last chapter. If all else fails in your search, start there.

USING WEB SEARCHERS

If you are new to the Internet, a Web Searcher is the best place to start searching for information. That's because it is the easiest and it can take you to Gopher and Archie sites as well.

There are plenty of Web Searchers available. Your access provider's program will almost certainly have a search command included. This is usually in the form of a button on which you click your mouse button. This takes you to a Web page which has a variety of methods of searching available. The search page allows you to enter a word or phrase for which you are looking. It then compiles another Web page with pointers or hot links direct to the information you are trying to find. The easiest way to see how this works is to look at a Web search.

Example of a Web Search

I wanted to find out some information about scientific research taking place in Brussels, Belgium. I started by looking for Brussels in the Web

Search page. This led me to over 500 further pages of information. Each one is listed as a hot link. By choosing one which was about the Faculty of Science at the Vrije University in Brussels I was able to find out that the Department of Biology has a research programme on oceanography. This led me to many more pages of information, including the name and address of the head of the department and his secretary's contact details. I was also able to find out which other researchers were collaborating with the department on oceanographic studies.

Finding that out took about five minutes and was just a local telephone call costing 4p. If I had wanted to find out this information in any other way, not only would I not have known where to begin, it would have taken several hours. Web searching is probably the most powerful information search tool you can find anywhere. It is worth using this method in preference to all others, unless you are looking for a specific file in which case Archie would be quicker.

HANDLING INTERNET INFORMATION

As you can see, you can very quickly get mountains of information from the Internet. This can be problematic as you will either run up large telephone bills, or run out of time to deal with all the material you get. You could also easily run out of hard disk storage space if you download a large number of files.

Planning and saving

The easy way out of this is to plan all searches in advance so that you can quickly get to the information you want. Also when you are searching, save your pages to your disk as you get them. You can then print them and read them without incurring on-line charges. This is particularly important if you pay your access provider by the hour, rather than a fixed monthly or annual fee. It is worthwhile scanning down pages, though, to see if there are further pointers or hot links to other pages that may be useful to you.

Many people will tell you to get information during low call charge periods, such as at weekends and during the evening period. However, this will not always save you money. Because these are the cheapest call periods they attract many more people to the Internet. That means access provider computers and all the leased lines connecting them can carry a large amount of **traffic** — people using the Internet. Naturally, when there is a lot of traffic, there are jams. Hence you can be waiting to connect to computers elsewhere on the Internet simply because of

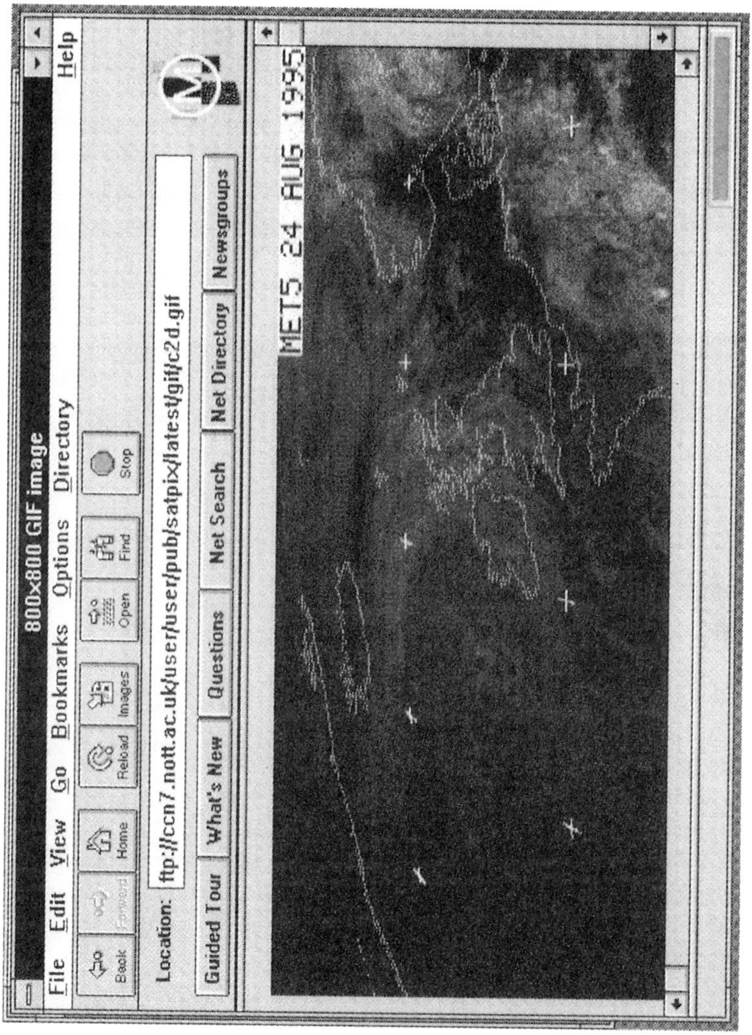

Fig. 8. You can download pictures.

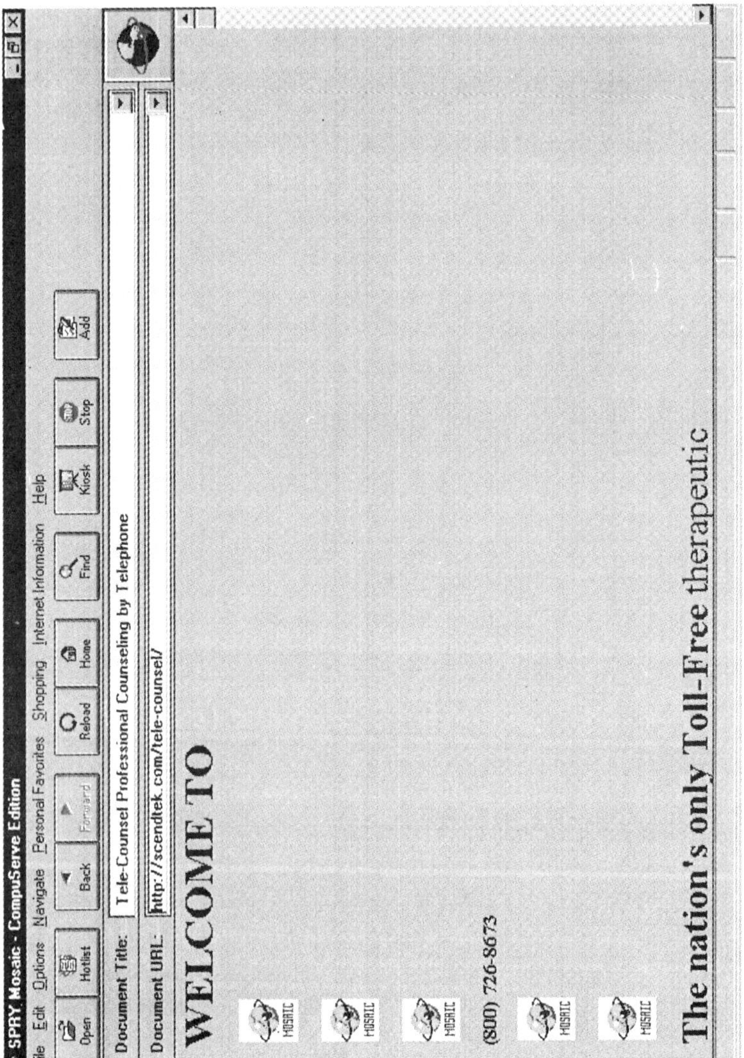

Fig. 9. If you switch off in-line graphics, your screen looks like this.

the volume of traffic. This can increase your call bill. Sometimes, if you know exactly what you are looking for, it is cheaper to connect to the Internet during peak call charge times. Your call will be short and you are unlikely to be delayed by excess Internet traffic.

This doesn't always work, though. If the computer which has the information you want is in another time zone, the traffic patterns will be different according to the local peak and cheap phone periods.

Plan your information searches and you will be able to work out when it will be cheapest to do your Internet access.

You can also speed up your web use and save costs by switching off "in-line" graphics in your browser program.

USING BOOKMARKS

Web browser programs allow you to mark specific pages of information that you particularly need to remember. You can then go direct to these pages when you want to in any other Internet session. This means you don't have to search again and waste valuable time.

You may think that if you have downloaded the information once, you need not do it again. However, Web pages are constantly being updated and you may want to check the page for the most up-to-date material. Having a **bookmark** that takes you direct to the relevant page is a great time and money saver and you should use them whenever possible. Different Internet access programs have different ways of using bookmarks, so whatever program you use, investigate the ways in which you can mark specific locations you want to return to.

LOCATING INFORMATION OFF-LINE

You don't have to connect to the Internet to find what you want. There are various methods you can use off-line. Each of the specialist Internet magazines listed in chapter 3 carries a directory as well as monthly updates. These directories are not extensive; there is far too much on the Internet to list in monthly magazines. However, the updates are very useful as they can point you to new and interesting Internet sites. One of the magazines, *.net*, also publishes a book-like directory called *The .net Directory*. This is sold in high street newsagents and is very useful since it lists many sites and also reviews them for you. In this way you can see whether a particular site is likely to be of use before you even start to incur telephone charges.

In addition to this directory there are more extensive, and more expensive, telephone directory-style books of Internet sites. Three popular ones are:

- *The Internet White Pages*
- *The Internet Yellow Pages*
- *The Internet Directory.*

You can scan through these directories, which have literally thousands of pages and tens of thousands of listings showing you exactly where to go for the information you want. It is worth buying one of these directories from your bookshop, but remember, the information was out of date before the printer finished the book! However, such directories are very useful starting points for locating information sites. You should have one.

CASE HISTORIES

Doctor launches new business

Keith is a doctor who has been dabbling on the Internet. He finds the extent of the information exciting and interesting. He decided to set up a part-time business offering information brokerage to fellow doctors. For a fee he finds out any kind of information that his colleagues want to know. He advertises in the medical press, offering information searches exclusively to doctors. They ask him to find out information on medical research around the world, new computer programs specific to the work of doctors and to extract material from the journals. He also gets asked to find out about the holiday opportunities in places that are due to have medical congresses! Keith offers a 48-hour turnaround. Doctors fax him with their requests, and he gets back to them within 48 hours. He does this by collecting all the information requests together, compiling them into sensible groups — journal requests, holiday information and so on — and then works out all his search terms. He dials up his access provider during the middle of the evening to reduce his call charges; most of the computers he will access are in America so he is calling during the daytime, when US traffic is lower. He calls every other day, which means that some people get their information back in a few hours, while others have to wait the full 48 hours. He charges £2 for every page of information he provides, which is considerably cheaper for the doctors than trying to get the information themselves. This part-time business is now so successful that Keith is considering giving up his medical work and establishing a full-time information service for doctors and other professionals.

Couple plan their holiday trip

Susan and David are going to the Caribbean next year for a three-week holiday. They want to find out information about the islands to decide where to go while they are away. They also want to find out about events in the area during the time they will be there. Using the Internet they have been able to search various Web pages for information and have now worked out where they will go and the events they will attend. It took them 30 minutes of connection time to find and download what they wanted. They did this during low call charge time so it only cost them 27p. The cheapest book they found was a year out of date and was £9.50.

CHECKLIST

- The Internet is an excellent way of getting information quickly and cheaply on almost any subject. However, you need a directory as a starting point and you then need to plan searches well in advance.
- As you get the information, store it on your computer and print it out for reading later; that way you will use the Internet efficiently and your phone bills will be kept low.
- The best way to search the Internet for information is to use a Web searcher.
- When you find good information sites of interest to you, make sure you use bookmarks for your computer to remember them by. That way you can return quickly to the areas of most use to you, again saving time and money.

DISCUSSION POINTS

1. What are the five principal ways of finding out about information that is available on the Internet?
2. What information areas are most likely to be of use to you?
3. How would you plan an information search?

6
Education via the Internet

If you just want to learn a bit more about a whole variety of topics you can use the information searching routines described in the last chapter. But if you want to really study, there are plenty of ways the Internet can help. Whether you want to learn a specific subject on a short course, or you want to take a degree or do postgraduate study, you can do it via the Internet. It is set to become the world's largest college — if it isn't already.

LEARNING AT A DISTANCE

Distance learning is not new. Correspondence courses and self study packs have been available for years. But the Internet provides you with much more than either of these traditional distance learning methods can.

Say you want to do some postgraduate business studies. You can do this with home-study courses from a number of universities and colleges; but you need to visit tutors regularly and you need to go to summer school.

You also, usually, end up taking the postgraduate diploma from the nearest college, for convenience. That may mean you are not taking the exact diploma you would like. Say the best diploma for your kind of work came from the Massachusetts Institute of Technology (MIT), and not the local college, it's hardly practical or economic to keep flying to the USA for tutorials each month! With the Internet you can do it — and at local call charges! That's because many institutions, including MIT, offer tutorials, classes and learning materials across the Internet. So too does the Open University in the UK, the University of Southampton, and Heriot-Watt University in Edinburgh. Naturally you have to pay course fees, but you would have to if you took a correspondence course.

The Internet's access to colleges

Some educationalists believe that the Internet is better than correspondence courses since it is almost like being at college, where slack work is noticed and you are obviously competing with other students. This provides the necessary motivation to learn. With correspondence courses you can pay your money up front and never open a book from that moment on; no one criticises you, suggests you should do the work or asks you searching questions. Usually all you get is a letter from the correspondence college offering you another course! I have a number of correspondence courses gathering dust which have never gone further than the first lesson.

With Internet courses, though, you are *in* college. You have contact with your lecturers, you even attend lectures that are broadcast across the Internet. You attend on-line tutorials with your fellow students. If you do not put the work in, it becomes obvious to everyone else during these tutorials. Although no one can see your face, your embarrassment is real, hence you are motivated to do better.

A new way of distance learning

- Learning at a distance using the Internet means you are much more likely to succeed, in comparison with other distance learning methods.

- It is also likely to be cheaper and you can access colleges around the world, rather than just the local ones.

FINDING OUT ABOUT EDUCATION ON THE INTERNET

You can use all of the search techniques discussed in chapter 5 to find out about educational sites around the Internet. However, there are two key addresses to visit if you want to find out about educational establishments and what they offer. To find out about British universities and colleges go to:

http://www.demon.co.uk/westlake/weblake/uk.html

If you want to find out about American universities go to:

http://www.lib.lsu.edu/general/scholar.html

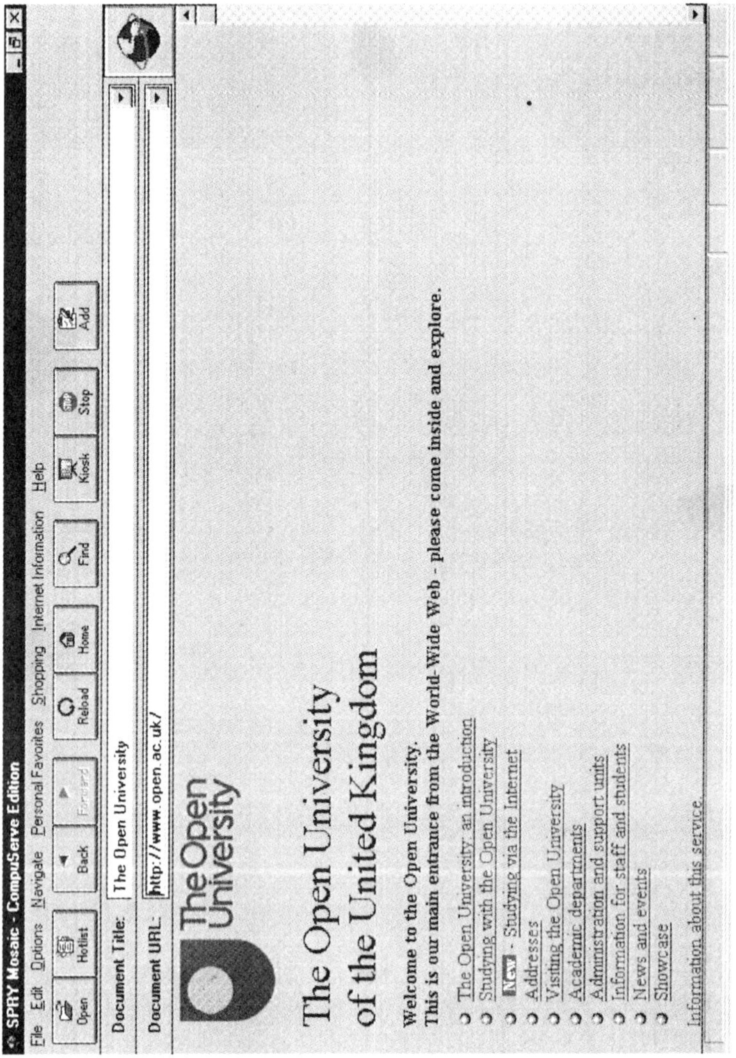

Fig. 10. You can gain degrees on the Internet.

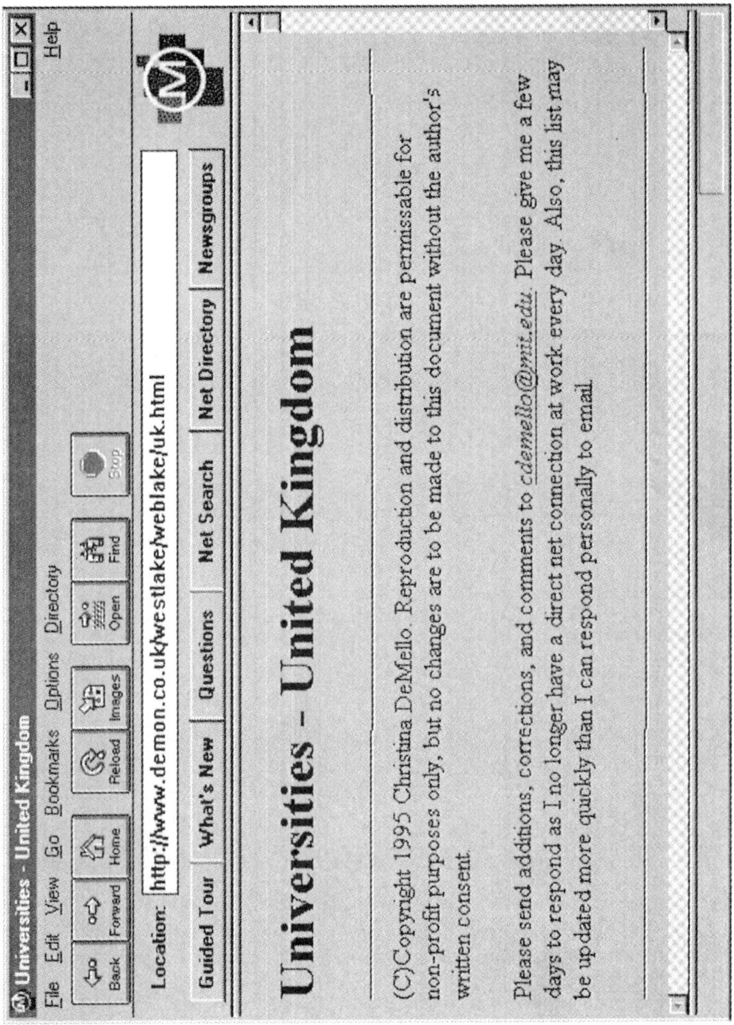

Fig. 11. Education is available from British universities.

This Web page will also provide you with hot links to other listings of universities and courses, including a list of universities and colleges elsewhere on the world. As always on the Internet, the addresses above must be typed *exactly* as you see them; that is, with all full stops in the right placc and with upper and lower case letters exactly as typed. If you make a mistake, say entering a capital letter when you should only enter a lower case letter, the address will not be found. This can be confusing to newcomers to the Internet; the rule is, type addresses exactly as you see them.

APPLYING FOR COURSES

You can apply for courses from Internet colleges using the Internet itself.

Filling in on-screen forms

Most of the colleges have on-screen forms that you fill in. You can go from one box on the form to the next by pressing the **tab** key on your keyboard. There will then be a box on the form, marked **submit**, which if you use your mouse button will send your application direct to the relevant college or university.

Other options

Sometimes, though, the software provided by your access provider does not allow you to use on-screen forms. If this is the case you will either be unable to see an on-screen form, or you will be unable to type anything into it. If you can't use an on-screen form, the Web page you are looking at will explain the options. Usually you can send the requested material direct to an email address. If your application is successful you will be informed by email, so always check your mailbox when you dial up.

Paying for courses

You will need to pay for many of the educational courses available over the Internet. Prices vary according to the extent of the course and the college that is providing the material. You can pay for courses by credit cards or cheques. If you pay by credit card, which is often more convenient, be careful. The Internet is a public place and it is comparatively easy for fraudsters to find out your credit card number and use it for themselves. Some people who request payment over the Internet using credit cards have security procedures in place; before you punch your credit card number into the Internet it's worth checking to see if the college offers security. If it does, this should be explained on the form you fill in.

PREPARING FOR INTERNET STUDIES

If your application for study is successful you will be sent all the relevant study materials. This usually includes lists of reading, your schedule of learning, timetables of tutorials and so on. Remember that even though you can get a great deal of reading material over the Internet your course may require you to buy textbooks, so your costs will often be higher than the course fees you pay. Also, you will naturally increase your telephone bill, so take this into account when budgeting for your education.

Another factor to take into account is the impact the studying will have on your family and social life. Although you would need to take this into account if you studied using traditional distance learning methods, the Internet way of studying can have *greater* impact. That's because you will be hogging the telephone line during the evenings. If your family want to make social calls they will find the line busy. Set yourself a timetable and let the rest of the family know when you will be studying and using the phone line to access the Internet. That way your studies won't be disturbed by family arguments!

BUYING TEXTBOOKS

You will almost certainly need additional textbooks for your studies, especially if you are taking a degree or doing postgraduate studies on the Internet. You can buy your books via the Internet, you don't even have to go out to the bookshop. If you lead a busy life, getting textbooks can be difficult and unless you live near to a university town most local bookshops do not stock degree-level texts. This means you have to travel to town, place an order, wait a couple of weeks, go back to town and collect your book. Using the Internet, things are much simpler and more convenient.

There are two ways to get your books.

Books published on the Internet

Some books are actually published on the Internet and you can download the full text. To see a list of books available for downloading to your computer go to:

http://www.cs.cmu.edu/Web/books.html

or

gopher://gopher.vt.edu

or

mailto:laura@editorial.com

These Internet sites provide you with books in electronic form which can sometimes work out cheaper than buying the book itself. However, you have to print out the book to be of any real use in studying. Having the book as a collection of loose-leaf pages may be less convenient than having a bound book. It is a matter of personal preference.

Buying actual books

You can, however, buy the actual books themselves. You can place an on-line order with a number of bookshops to have the book delivered by mail. This is particularly useful if a book is published in another country and not available in your own. Using the Internet bookshops means you can order difficult to obtain books like this. To order books try:

http://www.bookshop.co.uk/

or

http://www.blackwell.co.uk/bookshops/

If you use **CompuServe** or **E-world**, you will find additional electronic bookstores available to you. For instance, W H Smith has a bookshop on CompuServe.

STUDYING ON THE INTERNET

There are five key aspects to Internet study:

- on-line information
- on-line tutorials

- on-line essays
- email
- off-line study.

On-line information

Because your Internet connection allows you to obtain information on almost every subject from anywhere in the world, you have an advantage over students at traditional colleges and universities; you have access to the largest library in the world. Hence you can access all sorts of information on your chosen subject.

This takes some planning. You could spend all your study time surfing the net for information and not actually get any studying done. Proper planning of your studies will ensure you get the best out of the Internet while maintaining your schedule.

On-line tutorials

You will almost certainly take part in on-line tutorials. These are similar to Internet Relay Chat, explained in chapter 5. However, you will be using a 'string' or 'secret' channel, which means the conversation is private, only available to those taking part in the tutorial. Your college will advise you about the timing of these tutorials. It is worth letting the rest of the family know that you will be needing the telephone at a particular time; otherwise your phone line could be blocked and just like a normal student you will be late for the tutorial!

On-line essays and email

The essays you write and the project reports you complete will need to be submitted to your tutors and lecturers via the Internet. Usually you will do this by email. As always when sending material over the Internet, prepare it in advance and make sure it is finished before you dial up. Otherwise you will waste your connection time.

Also make sure you have the right email address; the best thing to do is store the relevant address in your **phone book**, which is part of your email program from your access provider.

Off-line study

Much of your work will be off-line study. You will either be reading textbooks, writing essays, or reading material you have downloaded from the Internet. In any event, this off-line work is likely to take up the bulk of your study time and you should plan for it. Don't get hooked into the Internet and lose that precious time, otherwise you will have wasted your course fees and increased your phone bill.

USING STUDENT GROUPS

Many colleges provide areas on the Internet for their students. These are basically newsgroups or Internet Relay Chat channels for the students who study using on-line methods. Often, these areas are only available to the students; access is denied to the lecturers and tutors. This means these areas become rather like the student bar at a university campus. You can go there to discuss anything you like, including whether you think you are being marked fairly or unfairly; you can swap notes and information on projects and so on. If you study using the Internet these student sites are worth a visit.

CASE HISTORIES

Martin studies for an MBA

Martin works in a high street bank and, although he has professional banking qualifications, he needs further proof of his management skills if he is to progress up the career ladder. He has two small children and wants to stay at home to help his wife look after them, so he can't give up work for a year and go and study — apart from the fact that he couldn't afford to. He decided to study for an MBA using distance learning techniques.

Martin enrolled for one course, but found that with the children about he wasn't motivated to meet the deadlines for his essays and project reports. The result was that he gave up the work and was upset by the waste of money. He was also concerned because if his bosses found out he had given up his studies, they could probably not think of him first when promotion was in the offing.

So Martin decided to take part in an Internet course. This has proved to be invaluable. He does study much more regularly than he did with the old course, because he takes part in the weekly tutorial on the Internet. This means that fellow students motivate each other to continue. He is now halfway through his course and his bosses are very pleased with his desire to improve his management skills with an MBA. Promotion looks likely, now his studies are progressing.

Tony studies art

Tony is a retired businessman who has always liked art. He is fond of impressionist paintings and also enjoys looking at 19th-century sculptures. However, his business career has meant he was never able to learn much about his hobby. Now he has retired he has taken up a short art course from an American university. He had looked at local evening classes, but none of them provided the right combination of studies to match his particular interests.

Tony was given a brand new personal computer with a CD-ROM and an Internet kit for his retirement present. While exploring the Internet one evening he discovered a course available in America which matched his precise interests. He enrolled straight away and has now almost finished his studies. He doesn't get a diploma, but he does get the satisfaction of having studied his hobby in some depth, with some of the world's leading experts. He couldn't have done that without the Internet.

CHECKLIST

- Studying on the Internet is an excellent way of distance learning that has significant advantages over traditional correspondence courses and self study kits.
- You can also get extra learning materials over the Internet that you couldn't get from local bookshops or from correspondence colleges.
- However, you need to plan your Internet studies carefully, particularly to ensure that the rest of the family understand your need to have access to the telephone at particular times.

DISCUSSION POINTS

1. Where would you start your search for suitable Internet courses?
2. Would you choose to download books or buy them via the Internet for home delivery?
3. How would you combine your home life with Internet studies?

7
Doing Business on the Internet

Large multinationals are already doing business on the Internet. Small businesses are also taking advantage of the Internet's facilities. One leading business commentator said, in mid-1995, that if a business isn't on the Internet by the end of this century, they won't be in business next century. In other words, you have just a few years to get your business on the Internet if you want to survive beyond the year 2000!

There are three principal aspects to Internet business:

- marketing
- sales
- communication.

MARKETING YOUR BUSINESS ON THE INTERNET

Many firms already use the Internet to market their business. They provide information about products and services, offer special promotions and allow users to view catalogues and so on. Whether you run a one-person business or are part of a large multinational public company, you can market your business on the Internet.

Your business on the World Wide Web

The best way to do this is using Web pages. Putting your business on the World Wide Web opens up all sorts of marketing possibilities that are not available easily using traditional marketing methods. You can, for instance, provide video footage of your product in action, or you can provide hot links to pages on other products you sell that might be compatible with the information the viewer is currently looking at. True, you can do the same kind of thing in a shop, but how can you do that in ordinary catalogues?

The Internet allows you to be much more creative in marketing and to reach potential customers anywhere in the world. With traditional marketing techniques you often have to restrict your efforts according to the budget. With the Internet your budget is the same no matter how many tens of thousands of people you reach. In other words, using Web pages as a way of marketing your business is one of the most cost effective methods you can find.

BUYING AND SELLING ON THE INTERNET

As you saw in chapter 6, you can buy books on the Internet, so companies are obviously using the Internet for sales. It's not just books you can buy over the Internet. You can purchase a whole host of different business and consumer products more conveniently and more quickly than trudging up and down the high street. This means that if you have products to sell, you can offer them to potential purchasers who want a more convenient method of shopping. The kinds of things already sold over the Internet include:

- antiques
- books
- car insurance
- cars
- CDs, records and tapes
- chocolates
- clothes
- computers
- consumer electronics
- drinks
- financial advice
- flowers
- food
- gifts
- household goods
- jewellery
- legal services
- lingerie
- magazines
- stationery
- telephones
- toys

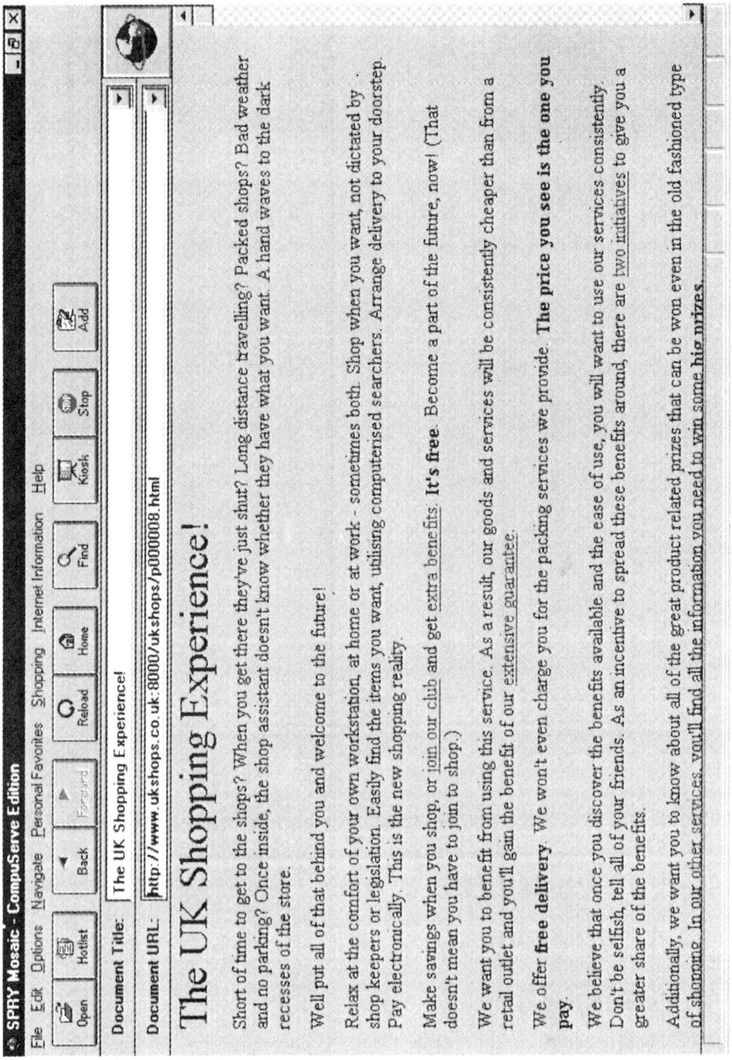

Fig. 12. Shopping on the Internet.

- travel tickets
- venison
- wine.

This is just a short collection of items on sale. There are various shopping 'malls' you can visit which allow you to see what's on offer and to place electronic orders for home delivery. If you want to see how other businesses sell on the Internet, visit these sites:

http://www.itl.net/barclaysquare/

or

http://www.ukshops.co.uk:8000/

or

http://www6.internet.net

There are plenty of other shopping sites on the Internet and new ones are being added daily. You need to use Web searches if you are looking for particular products.

Because many businesses are selling products and services over the Internet, you may need to investigate how your business could benefit from having an Internet presence. Later in this chapter we will look at the possibilities.

COMMUNICATING WITH BUSINESS COLLEAGUES

The Internet is an excellent way of performing business communications. As was explained in chapter 4, there are a number of advantages for businesses to communicate on the Internet. These include:

- reduced costs

- improved efficiency

- time savings.

If you are in any kind of business you can achieve these benefits from the Internet's communications capabilities. If you haven't read chapter

4, you should do so to see how the communication facilities could improve your business life.

You can communicate more efficiently, cheaply and quickly with colleagues, customers and suppliers using the Internet than in any other way.

ESTABLISHING AN INTERNET PRESENCE

If you want to market your business, or you want to sell your products or services, you will need an Internet presence. The best way to do this is with Web pages. However, your pages need to be available round the clock, seven days a week, if they are to be viewed by anyone using the Internet. You can achieve this in two ways:

- leased lines
- space rental.

Getting leased lines

If you want an extensive Internet presence it may work out more cost-effective to have leased lines installed. These lines are permanently connected to your computer, which is left permanently switched on. You will need a computer dedicated to the sole job of providing information on the Internet.

Such a computer is known as a **server**; you will see advertisements in the computer press for Web Servers. These are powerful personal computers with appropriate software to allow you to produce Web pages and make them available over the Internet. Your Web Server then becomes one of the many thousands of machines permanently connected in the international network that is the Internet. There are two key problems with this approach.

Costs

A leased line will cost from about £10,000 a year to rent, plus you will need to buy the Web Server, which will be about £4,000. If you want to go along this route the main providers of leased lines for the Internet in the UK are:

Pipex on 0500 47 47 39.

Computer expertise

In addition you will need someone who has some degree of computer expertise. Not only will this person need to understand the intricacies of attaching the computer to a leased line and to the worldwide network, they will also need some design skills. That's because the pages on the World Wide Web are much like magazine pages. They include headlines and graphics as well as the text and the hot links to other information elsewhere on the Internet.

In addition to these design skills, the computer whizz-kid also needs a bit of computer programming knowledge. That's because the pages for the Web are not prepared using a 'what you see is what you get' approach. In other words, the pages as they appear to you on the Internet are not as they appear to the person who produced them. Instead, the text and information is coded using a computer language known as **Hypertext Mark-up Language** or **HTML** — you will have seen these letters in some of the Internet addresses in this book. It is not difficult computer language, but you need to be confident in using the codes if your pages are to look attractive and bring custom.

Renting space

One way out of the problems of creating Web pages and the costs of leased lines is to rent space on someone else's Web Server. Many access providers offer this service and there are some companies which only provide space on their own machines attached to leased lines. In this way they recoup the costs of their equipment by renting space on their computer.

Most companies rent space according to the size of the files you will need. These are measured in megabytes and for up to 5Mb most companies charge around £25 per month. The more space you use, the lower the cost per megabyte.

What companies offer

Some companies will take your text and design your Web pages for you, others will expect you to provide the computer files in HTML format. If you don't want to get involved in HTML programming, get a space rental company that will do the work for you; sometimes they will charge extra for this, of course.

If you do choose the space rental route, it is best to work with a local supplier. That way you can visit their office, make sure that they are doing the work and generally feel comfortable about the handling of your account.

If you are to use the Internet as a means of marketing and selling you need to be sure that the space rental company you use is up to the job.

Ask the same questions of them as you would your access provider, as outlined in chapter 3. In fact, if you can, it is best to use your access provider as your Web 'publisher', providing space on their own Web Server.

FINDING OUT MORE ABOUT HTML

If you do want to produce your own Web pages, it isn't difficult. In fact when exploring the Internet you will find that many individuals have **home pages** which just give some details about their background and experience and a few personal comments. You can then email them by using a hot link direct to their mailbox.

If individuals can produce Web pages from their back bedroom, there is no reason why people in business cannot produce their own. In fact you might even enjoy it! There are plenty of books about HTML and plenty of information on it on the Internet. However, I have found that the book which has been most useful to me is *Teach Yourself Web Publishing with HTML in a Week* by Laura Lemay (SAMS Publishing, ISBN 0-672-30667-0). You can order this from the on-line bookshops whose details are in chapter 6.

LAUNCHING YOUR BUSINESS ON THE INTERNET

Having Web pages is one thing, but you need to let people know you are there! It may take some time before people stumble across your pages. Tell all your customers, suppliers and every one of your contacts that you are now available on the Internet. Also let all the on-line directories of businesses know that your pages are now available. You can discover indexes of directories using the Web Search tools available in your access program.

You will also want to let certain key sites on the Internet know of your presence. Make sure you post an email message to the lists appropriate to your business. You can do this easily using the Web page of the list; there is always a hot link direct to the administrator's mailbox. All you need do is post a message saying what your Web page address is. It's a good idea to post a message to the following Web page:

http://www.directory.net/

This is an index of commercial services available on the Internet. Anyone wanting to find out about particular service availability is likely to search this page. If your Web page is listed you are likely to receive visitors to your promotional material. If it isn't listed, hard luck!

Also get your Web pages listed in all the relevant directories. This includes all the Web magazines and the 'telephone' directory books which index the Internet.

In addition to the magazines listed in chapter 3, make sure you tell *Net Guide*. This is America's leading Internet magazine and also has an international circulation. *Net Guide* can be contacted on:

http://techweb.cmp.com/net

or at

netmail@netguide.cmp.com

As soon as you have an Internet presence, let as many people know as possible using these techniques, otherwise your Web page could be a well kept secret!

TAKING ORDERS ON THE INTERNET

If you are to sell things on the Internet, or even just provide further information, you need a way for your customers to get in touch with you. There are a number of options available. These include:

- email
- Web forms
- file transfer
- phone
- fax
- post.

email orders

Taking orders by email is clearly possible since every Internet user can send email. However, it is not the most convenient. The customer has to type in their order and make sure they send it to the right mailbox. You can boost the accuracy of ordering by ensuring you have a hot link on your Web page direct to your mailbox. Although email ordering is simple, it does mean that the customer has to do a lot of the work for themselves and this could be off-putting.

Web forms

These are by far the most convenient way for customers to place orders since they can simply tick the products or services they want. They then just press the submit button and their order is sent, together with their Internet address details. It's straightforward and very easy. The only problem is that not everyone on the Internet has the ability to use on-screen forms, so you are potentially limiting your supply of customers.

File transfer

Since everyone on the Internet has the ability to transfer files from one computer to another using FTP, they can send orders to your computer this way. This has an advantage in that they can send other files with their order. Say your company offers personalised goods such as a diary with initials on the front, people could use a scanner to scan in their signature and they could send this file together with their order. You could then print their signature on the front of the diary, instead of initials.

Phone, fax, post

These are the traditional methods of order taking and you should make these available to your Internet customers. In spite of the fact that there are many Internet addicts, some of them are still wary of ordering goods and services over the Internet. If you don't provide them with alternative methods of ordering, you could lose their custom.

PROCESSING ORDERS FROM THE INTERNET

If you are taking orders from Internet users you need to work out how you will integrate these within your current ordering system. You also need to work out who will be responsible for downloading orders and how frequently.

Another consideration when doing business on the Internet is how you will provide customer receipts. Also, how will you keep customers informed of progress with their orders if there is any delay? You should take all these factors into account when starting to do business on the Internet. Do not set up Web pages with sophisticated ordering capabilities if you haven't worked out how you will process those orders.

Collecting the money

There are a number of ways you can collect the money from people who order via the Internet. The most straightforward for the customer is a credit card or debit card. However, you may not be able to process credit card transactions, so you may want payment by cheque or bankers draft.

Large businesses and government departments may not want to pay when ordering and will expect you to work using a purchase order scheme.

If you are to maximise your business on the Internet you should really accept all forms of payment, otherwise you could lose customers to the competition which can accept payments in a variety of methods.

Accepting credit cards

Having forms with spaces for credit card details is the easiest way for your customers to pay. You can increase their confidence in security by having various registration schemes available that means their credit card number is protected from Internet fraudsters.

You can do this by having new customers fill in a registration form, which automatically allocates them a customer number. They then telephone you with their credit card details. Whenever they order they quote their customer number and you can automatically allocate the payment to a particular credit card number.

Alternatively, they can complete the order over the Internet but later on fax over their credit card details.

Another method is to use Web browser software that provides for the secure transmission of credit card and other confidential information. On your order form you could provide a hot link to an Internet site that provides these 'safe' browsers. Your customers can then easily download the appropriate program and then re-order safely.

Accepting cheques

You can collect the money using standard cheques or bankers drafts. However, you need to make it clear on your order form that orders will not be delivered until the cheques have cleared. Otherwise you could find yourself with a bounced cheque and the customer could be on the other side of the planet. Chasing up such payments can be very costly indeed.

Purchase orders

If you are prepared to deal with firms which buy with a purchase ordering system you will need a comprehensive credit checking facility. Happily, there are ways you can check credit status using the Internet and other on-line services, such as E-world or CompuServe. Your order forms should make it clear that if someone wants to buy a product using a purchase order, the order will not be processed until credit references have been approved. Otherwise you could find yourself chasing money from some far-flung place.

CASE HISTORIES

Book publisher expands market

Magnificent Books is a general book publishing company that provides highly illustrated, non-fiction titles aimed at the higher end of the market. Their books are expensive and appeal to people who love having good-looking books strewn around the house to impress their visitors. For some time Magnificent Books has had a problem in that although its products sell well, they can't seem to expand the market and get higher sales volumes on their titles.

The owner decided to try the Internet as a way of selling. She set up a Web page that described the kinds of books on offer. Each book also had its own Web page that gave pictures of the book itself, selected illustrations and details of the text and the author. In addition, people could download the entire text themselves to print out. The idea was that once people read the text they would prefer to have the real book, particularly as they had already seen some of the lavish illustrations. There was also an order form for each book so that people could buy the book direct from the publisher.

Not only was this highly acceptable to the readers, it was better for the publisher since no discounts had to be given to distributors and booksellers. More profit per book sold was made using the Internet sales system. Magnificent Books has had a magnificent year. Their sales have increased and they have found an extra source of profit.

Mail order firm invents new catalogue

A traditional mail order supplier of household goods has put its entire catalogue on the Internet. However, unlike the normal printed catalogue, this one has hot links to associated products. There are also spoken descriptions from customers who have praised individual products. Some products also have video of them in action. The sounds and videos can be easily accessed by hot links on the catalogue's Web pages. The company has found that by linking together associated products they have increased sales; people who would normally have bought only one product from the catalogue are buying additional ones that would have been harder to associate using the printed version.

CHECKLIST

- Business is going to be increasingly performed over the Internet. There probably is not one business that couldn't be performed over the Internet.
- The Internet provides for greater business efficiency and increases business opportunities.
- If your business is to thrive it needs to consider an Internet presence.
- If you do have information about your business on the Internet, plan your presence carefully and, unless you are happy with computers, get a local Internet access provider to produce your pages and provide you with Internet space.

DISCUSSION POINTS

1. What are the benefits your business could derive from an Internet presence?
2. Are there any reasons why your business could not be on the Internet?
3. What is the most cost effective way for your business to have an Internet presence?

8
How to Behave on the Internet

In the same way that there are 'rules' about the way you write to people, phone them or do business with them, there are rules about the way you behave on the Internet. This concept is called **netiquette**. It is a hotch-potch collection of things you should and shouldn't do if your Internet work is to be of benefit to you and other users.

GETTING EMAIL RIGHT

One of the most infuriating things about direct mail is getting the same unsolicited piece of mail from the same company three or four times. That happens when their mailing lists are not checked properly. Equally, when you get unsolicited email a number of times you will also be upset. Hence the first way of ensuring that you don't upset other users is to make sure that your email is correctly addressed. To do this:

- check all email addresses before sending
- check your address book for duplicates.

Using shorthand

Another problem with email is getting long, unnecessary messages that could have been replaced with a short missive. Wherever possible, use the shorthand described in chapter 4. This will make your emailing much more acceptable to the recipients.

Mailbombing

Finally, do not do what is known as 'mailbombing'. This is where you send enormous messages to people that take up a large amount of disk space and a great deal of time to download. Victims of mailbombs have received messages like: 'I thought you would like to read the attached'.

This short message is then followed by the complete works of Shakespeare, taking up a vast amount of space and lots of connection time. Only when you receive the file do you discover that you didn't want it or need it. Such mailbombing is outlawed and if Internet access providers discover who does this kind of thing they close down their accounts.

Capitals

Finally, when sending messages by email only SHOUT if you have to. Sending material in all capitals is known as **shouting** and it is perceived as being rude, unless you need to shout to emphasise something.

GETTING IT RIGHT IN NEWSGROUPS

In the same way as email needs to be concise, so too do messages in newsgroups. There is nothing more infuriating to other people accessing the newsgroup than finding a rambling message from someone who is not really contributing to the discussion. If you have something to say, do it as concisely as possible. If you have nothing to contribute, keep your keyboard untouched!

Spamming

One particular problem that can occur in newsgroups is similar to mailbombing. This is called **spamming**. It occurs when people send a message to every newsgroup on the Internet. This was done in a famous case when a law firm advertised their services everywhere on the Internet. The result was every newsgroup had space taken up on the computer for something it didn't need. It also meant that Internet users had increased connection time which was unnecessary, and there was increased traffic on the network making everything slow for all users. This law firm had its Internet account closed. The rule is:

- only send messages to newsgroups and newsgroup members who really can benefit from the information.

For instance, if you have a question about the availability of boats for hire in Southampton, don't send the message to every newsgroup in the hope that someone might know the answer. Instead, send it to the appropriate recreation newsgroup. Otherwise you may find your life on the Internet is short-lived.

Flaming

If you see messages you do not like in newsgroups and want to attack the message sender, it is a good idea to do this direct through their email address rather than through the newsgroup. If you do send a newsgroup message it will be read by other people accessing the group. Sending personal attacks to a newsgroup is known as **flaming** and you will be seen as an irritant by other users.

UNDERSTANDING OTHER ASPECTS OF NETIQUETTE

Observing copyright

Much of what you get from the Internet is protected by copyright — books, magazines, images, etc. When using the Internet the providers of the material have given you the option to download the material for your own use. It is illegal for you to even photocopy the material you get or print it out more than once. Similarly, it is illegal for you to upload copyright material to the Internet without permission of the owner of the copyright. Remember:

- everything that is written down — even your shopping list — is protected by copyright.

Just because the Internet is international don't think you won't get caught. There is an international agreement on copyright and every country which has signed this agreement — that's all of the Western World plus many countries in the Third World — are constantly policing breaches of copyright.

Death threats

Just as it is illegal to send a death threat through the mail or over the telephone, it is illegal to send death threats over the Internet. Someone sent a death threat via the Internet to Bill Clinton's mailbox at the Whitehouse. The perpetrator was jailed for the offence.

FAQs

These are **frequently asked questions** and most sites on the Internet have them. They provide answers to the most commonly asked questions about the particular area of the Internet you are exploring. It is always worth reading FAQs as they will point the way to good behaviour in the section of the Internet in which you are working.

Libel

Just as it is an offence to defame someone in print, it is wrong to do so on the Internet. Because the Internet is essentially a 'publication' you will commit libel, rather than slander which attracts low penalties. If you libel someone on the Internet you could be prosecuted, not only by the person libelled, but also by your access provider and other people who provide Internet services, since you will have breached your agreement with them. If you don't understand the intricacies of the libel laws, restrict your comments about other people to facts that can be substantiated.

Pornography

Although there are pornographic images available on the Internet, it should be obvious that if you access them you shouldn't pass them on via the Internet to other people. They may not want to receive them. Equally, if you have pornographic images you want to 'upload' to the Internet, make sure you only send them to the relevant pornographic sites.

Most people do not use the Internet for pornography and if you think this is all there is to it you are very much mistaken. You will have a short-lived life on the Internet if you distribute pornography outside the relevant areas.

CENSORING AREAS OF THE INTERNET

If you have a computer at home you may want to protect your children from certain aspects of the system. Not only could this be pornography, you may want to stop them using the Internet to buy things.

You may also want to stop them from making excessively long periods of access.

If you have Internet access in your business, you may want to make similar restrictions for your staff. Until relatively recently access to the Internet was unrestricted. However there are some ways in which you can 'censor' the Internet.

Restrictions from your access provider

Choose an access provider which does some censoring for you. There are a number of access providers, for instance, who will not allow their computers to connect to newsgroups that begin with alt.sex. In this way you avoid much of the pornography that circulates. If you have youngsters who use your computer for Internet work, you might want to consider using an access provider who applies some restrictions. When you apply for an account, ask what level of access is provided and whether or not any censoring takes place.

Restrictions applied through programs

Another way to censor the Internet is to use a program that either intercepts certain words typed in from the keyboard or requires passwords from individual users. The most well known of these programs are called:

- **Net Nanny**
- **FireWall.**

Net Nanny was developed in Canada and checks the input from the keyboard. It monitors for particular words that you choose in advance, such as 'sex' or 'racial hatred'. If these words are typed in, the computer is disconnected from the Internet. For more information on Net Nanny call Leaf Distribution. Tel: (01256) 707777. Or:

email sales@leaf.co.uk

FireWall is aimed mainly at business users and provides certain levels of access to the Internet for particular users. It also provides an auditing and logging system so you can monitor which employee is doing what kind of work on the Internet. For more information on FireWall call Integralis. Tel: (01734) 306060. Or:

email info@integralis.co.uk

CHECKLIST

- If the Internet is to succeed people need to behave properly in the same way they are expected to behave in society generally.
- Many laws which apply to ordinary publishing also apply to the Internet; it is sometimes easier to see if you have committed an offence on the Internet than with traditional methods because it is so public.
- It is possible to censor the Internet and if you have children who use your computer this is a good idea.

- It is also a good idea for businesses to ensure that their telephone bills are not unnecessarily increased.

- If you want to know more about Netiquette use your Web browser to open the following URL:

ftp://ftp.sura.net

9
Planning for the Future

One thing is sure, the Internet is here to stay. But what it will be like in the future is still an area of massive speculation. What seems certain is that it will be more popular than ever and will offer even more possibilities than you ever dreamed of — at least if big communications companies get behind it, which they are increasingly doing.

Another virtual certainty is that the Internet will change. It *is* changing perceptibly each month, so how it will appear by the end of the century is anyone's guess. But you need to think about the potential impact the changes will have now, if your investment in the Internet is to be profitable. If you buy a set of equipment now, only to find that in a year's time your enjoyment of the Internet is limited, you will have to start again. One of the areas in which this has been proven time and time again is when people have bought comparatively slow modems to save some money. They then find the modems too slow to usefully access things like the video images or colour catalogues from on-line stores. As was stated in chapter 2, buy the biggest, fastest, etc and you will be able to enjoy the best of the Internet for some time to come.

But what if the Internet changes out of all recognition?

PREDICTING THE FUTURE

To be sure you know what is happening with the development of the Internet you really do need to keep up-to-date. One way is to buy a specialist Internet magazine each month. Not only does this help you keep up with developments, it will also update your directory of useful sites.

Another way to keep up-to-date is to go direct to some of the Internet sites which deal with the Internet itself. Some useful ones include:

ftp://nic.merit.edu

http://www.internic.net/scout.report

You will find all sorts of hints in these areas and in the magazines about the way things are going. You will be surprised at the rapidity of the developments, and if you want to get the most out of the Internet you really do need to keep yourself well-informed and as up-to-date as possible.

WHAT IS LIKELY TO HAPPEN?

There are some key things we already know about that are likely to happen within the next few years on the Internet. These include:

- access direct from telephones
- access via your television
- cheap telephone calls
- live video conferencing.

Access direct from telephones

Companies are already developing small devices that will sit next to your telephone. Their only computing power will be to access the Internet. They will not be able to perform any other computing functions, so if you want to manipulate the data you extract you will need to transfer it to a computer.

However, the developers believe there is a market for this device. They think that some people are put off the Internet because it is a 'computer thing'. If the computer link can be removed and the Internet access device can be turned into a customer electronic item, the developers believe, this will dramatically increase the success of the Internet. They are probably right. Look out for these devices on sale during 1996.

Access via your television

One television manufacturer is already looking into incorporating Internet access through the TV set. The idea would be that you would use your remote control to access Internet pages, in much the same way as you use the device to view Teletext pages now. If this technological leap happens — and it most certainly will — the Internet will become accessible to almost everyone in the land. This will mean that business will be even keener to get on the Internet. In fact the ever-increasing consumerisation of Internet access means that it is even more likely to become important in our everyday lives.

Cheap telephone calls

Many people on the Internet are already benefiting from the ability to make cheap telephone calls. Because your connection is most likely to be made with a local access provider, you will only be charged local call rates. Providing your computer has the appropriate sound board installed, you can download software from the Internet which will allow this board to be used essentially as a telephone. This means your computer can then dial up other people, anywhere in the world, via the Internet. Your call, even to Australia, is via the Internet and hence you can talk at local rates. Watch for this becoming ever more popular in the future.

Live video conferencing

In much the same way as you can make cheap telephone calls on the Internet you can already make **video calls**, providing you have the appropriate extras in your computer and a camera attached. At the moment the video is slow and jerky, but computer engineers should have that cracked in about a year or so. This means that you could hold international video business conference calls for the price of a local call.

CHECKLIST

- You need to keep up-to-date with what is happening in the world of the Internet if you are to get the most out of it.
- If you don't your enjoyment could be spoiled in the future.
- Or you could waste your money now by purchasing equipment that won't be able to cope with expected developments in the future.

Appendix: Finding Access Providers

Up-to-date lists of local access providers are contained in the specialist Internet magazines available from newsagents. The magazines are listed in chapter 3.

However, there are some access providers which have a nationwide network of Points of Presence (POPs). Those listed below are the most well known. This list is not exhaustive and there are bound to be other companies which now provide a nationwide POP, but did not at the time of writing. Inclusion in this list does not mean the suppliers are recommended or approved in any way.

BBC Networking Club. Tel: (0181) 576 7799. Fax: (0181) 993 6281.

CompuServe. Tel: 0800 289458.

Delphi. Tel: (0171) 757 7150. Fax: (0171) 757 7160.

Demon. Tel: (0181) 349 0063. Fax: (0181) 349 0309.

Direct Connection. Tel: (0181) 317 0100. Fax: (0181) 317 3886.

Eunet. Tel: (01227) 266466. Fax: (01227) 266477.

Future Connect. Tel: (01233) 566950. Fax: (01223) 566951.

Greennet. Tel: (0171) 713 1941. Fax: (0171) 833 1169.

Microsoft Network. Tel: 0800 750800.

PC User Group. Tel: (0181) 863 1191. Fax: (0181) 863 6095.

Pipex. Tel: 0500 47 47 39. Fax: (01223) 250121.

Rednet Online. Tel: (01494) 513333. Fax: (01494) 443374.

UK Online. Tel: (01749) 333333.

Glossary

Access provider. The company (sometimes called a service provider) that sells you a method of getting your computer connected to the rest of the Internet.

Archie. One of the methods of searching for files on the Internet.

Baud. The number of pieces of computer information transmitted per second.

BPS. Bits per second, transmitted by your modem.

Client. The computer program you are using to do the particular work on the Internet you want.

Cyberspace. A term from a novel meaning the entire world of computers linked together.

Dial up.Connecting to the Internet using your computer and a modem to make a call to your access provider.

Domain. A description of where a computer is somewhere in the world. It identifies a particular part of the Internet.

Download. To transfer information to your computer from another one on the Internet.

Email. Mail sent electronically between two computers.

Email address. Your address on the Internet. The specific pointer to you, just like your home address in the postal system.

FAQ. Shorthand for frequently asked questions.

Flame. To abuse people publicly on the Internet.

FTP. File transfer protocol: the way computers talk to each other to transfer information across the Internet.

Gopher. A searching system for finding things on the Internet.

Host. The computer your access company uses to connect you to the Internet.

Hostname. Name given to the host computer.

HTML. Hypertext mark-up language used to create Web pages.

HTTP. Stands for 'hypertext transfer protocol'. Hypertext is a computerised method of improving the way you can use the system.

IP. Internet protocol: An internationally agreed set of computer instructions that ensure machines on the Internet can connect to each other and transfer information.

IRC. Internet relay chat: live discussions on the Internet.

Leased line. Permanently open telephone line connecting a computer to the Internet.

Logging in. Entering your user details to let you access the system.

Mailbox. A storage area on your access provider's computer (host) in which information addressed to your email address is stored.

Modem. Device that connects your computer to the telephone system and performs the necessary translation of the signals.

Mosaic. One of the most common Web browser programs.

Netiquette. Standards of behaviour expected from Internet users.

Netscape. One of the most common Web browser programs.

Newsgroup. Specific area of the Internet for discussing a particular subject.

POP. Point of presence locations where you can access the Internet from a particular access provider.

POP3. Nothing to do with point of presence, but a method for sending electronic mail messages. Stands for post office protocol number 3.

Post. To send an email message or a message to a newsgroup.

PPP. Point to point protocol: the way in which two computers at different sites talk to each other.

PSTN. Public switched telephone network: the telephone system!

Server. A large computer that is one of the main machines on the Internet.

Service provider. An access provider.

SLIP. Serial line Internet protocol: one of the ways in which connected computers talk to each other.

Smiley. Facial expression produced by typewriter characters to indicate your mood to the recipient of your message.

TCP. Transmission control protocol: the computer's programs method of communication with the Internet.

Telnet. A means of connecting directly to other computers on the Internet.

Upload. To transfer information from your computer to another one on the Internet.

URL. Shorthand for an 'address', that is the location of the material you are looking for. Stands for uniform resource locator and can be used to identify an individual computer, or a particular piece of information on a specific computer.

WWW. World Wide Web, sometimes called W3.

Further Reading

All You Need to Know about UK Internet Service Providers, Davey Winder (Future Publishing, 1995)

Guerilla Marketing on the Internet, Jay Conrad Levinson and Charles Rubin (Piatkus, 1995)

How to Manage Computers at Work, Graham Jones (How To Books, 1993)

Internet Explorer Kit, Adam Engst and Bill Dickson (Hayden Books, 1994)

Internet Starter Kit, Adam G Engst (Hayden Books, 1994)

Launching a Business on the Web, David Cook and Deborah Sellers (Que Corporation, 1995)

New Riders' Official Internet Directory, Christine Maxwell (New Riders Publishing, 1994)

Paperless Publishing, Colin Hayes (Windcrest/McGraw-Hill, 1994)

Success with the Internet, Allen Wyatt (Jamsa Press, 1994)

Teach Yourself Web Publishing with HTML in a Week, Laura Lemay (SAMS Publishing, 1995)

The Internet Business Guide, Rosalind Resnick and Dave Taylor (SAMS Publishing, 1994)

The Internet Unleashed, Steven Bang (SAMS Publishing, 1994)

The Internet Yellow Pages, Harley Hahn (Osborne/McGraw-Hill, 1994)

The UK Internet Book, Sue Schofield (Addison Wesley, 1995)

MAGAZINES

All the computer magazines cover the Internet. The specialist magazines are all available from newsagents. Larger branches of W H Smith and Menzies include all the Internet magazines. You may have to order them from smaller branches. The leading Internet magazines are:

.net

Internet

Internet and Comms Today

Net Guide

NetUser

What Net

Wired

ON-LINE FURTHER READING

ftp://ftp.eff.org

ftp://ftphost.nwnet.net

ftp://nic.merit.edu

ftp://world.std.com

gopher://noonan@msus1.msus.edu

Index

How To Manage Computers at Work
Graham Jones

Here is a practical step-by-step guide which puts the business needs of the user first. It discusses why a computer may be needed, how to choose the right one and instal it properly; how to process letters and documents, manage accounts, and handle customer and other records and mailing lists. It also explains how to use computers for business presentations, and desktop publishing. If you feel you should be using a computer at work, but are not sure how to start, then this is definitely the book for you. . . and you won't need an electronics degree to start! 'Bags of information in a lingo we can all understand. I strongly recommend the book.' *Progress/NEBS Management Association*. Graham Jones has long experience of handling personal computers for small business management. The Managing Director of a desktop publishing company, he is also author of *How to Start a Business from Home* and *How to Publish a Newsletter* in this Series.

£8.99, 160pp, 1 85703 078 8.

How to Do Your Own P.R.
Ian Phillipson

Public relations is one of the best ways of promoting any organisation, business or event. It is not as costly as advertising, and properly used can produce far better results. This new book provides a really practical step-by-step guide to doing your own P.R., whether you want a one-off press release, or a more formal and wide ranging campaign. It shows how to recognise and create stories that interest the media, how to write and lay out press releases, how to be interviewed by the press, as well as providing a bank of proven ideas for public relations stories. The book is complete with helpful checklists and realistic case studies. Ian Phillipson is an experienced public relations consultant with a range of clients in the public and private sectors.

£8.99, 144pp illus. 1 85703 145 8.

How to Sell Your Business
Robert Ziman

Are you thinking of selling your business? Perhaps you feel it is time for a change, or retirement beckons, or your personal circumstances have changed. Whatever the reasons, you will certainly want to get the best deal. But how do you market a business? What about the timing, method and costs? What about confidentiality, and negotiating with prospective buyers? Written by a business transfer agent with a lifetime's experience, this book shows you step-by-step how to manage the whole process from the beginning, through setbacks, and towards a satisfactory outcome. It is complete with many examples, checklists, sample documents and other essential information to set you on your way.

£9.99, 160pp illus. 1 85703 119 9.

How to Communicate at Work
Ann Dobson

Things only get done properly at work if everyone communicates effectively — whatever their individual role in the organisation. This very practical step-by-step guide gets to the very basics of good communication — what it is and why we need it, how to speak and listen, how to ask and answer questions, how to take messages and use the telephone; how to liaise, negotiate, persuade, offer advice and accept criticism; how to stand up for yourself, dealing with shyness, a difficult boss or angry customer; how to use and understand body language properly, how to copy with visitors, how to store and present information, how to use the English language correctly — and a great deal more, illustrated throughout with examples and case studies. Written by an experienced office staff trainer this book will be a real help to all young people starting a new job, or older individuals returning to work after time away.

£7.99, 192pp illus. 1 85703 103 2.

How to Start Word Processing
Ian Phillipson

In the modern world an ability to wordprocess is a valuable, even essential, skill. It opens up new career opportunities, allows you to do your job so much better, and to complete all kinds of assignments far more quickly and effectively. Even if you know little or nothing about modern technology, this book will help you, because it deals with basic principles. If you want to design and print out simple letters and documents, produce mailshots, or explore desk top publishing, then this is the book for you, complete with case studies and checklists to help you on your way. Ian Phillipson is an experienced DTP and business consultant, with a range of business and professional clients in both the public and private sectors.

£8.99, 124pp illus. 1 85703 156 3.

How to Understand Finance at Work
Peter Marshall

Are you in the dark about financial decisions? Are you concerned that those in charge are not making financial plans in the most responsible way? Using plain English, this book demystifies the whole subject of finance in any private or public sector organisation — where it comes from, what it is for, how it can be used, how current and capital projects are managed, and how sound financial decisions should be reached. Equip yourself to play a better role in understanding and managing finance in your own organisation. 'Should be of interest to employees wanting to gain a knowledge of how a company can be affected by its finances.' *Mind Your Own Business.*

£8.99, 150pp illus. 1 85703 086 9.